Fay Jones

A 20 Year Retrospective

Boise Art Museum
August 31 - October 27, 1996

Exhibition Organized by
Sandy Harthorn
Curator of Exhibitions

Essays by
Regina Hackett
Sondra Shulman

Tour Itinerary

Boise Art Museum
Boise, Idaho
August 31 - October 27, 1996

Washington State University Museum of Art
Pullman, Washington
January 14 - February 23, 1997

Seattle Art Museum
Seattle, Washington
March 20 - July 22, 1997

This publication has been prepared in conjunction with *Fay Jones: A 20 Year Retrospective,* an exhibition organized by Sandy Harthorn for the Boise Art Museum and a subsequent tour.

The exhibition and publication have been made possible by support from Stoel Rives LLP, Attorneys; Montgomery Watson Americas, Inc., Engineers; Grover/Thurston Gallery; Laura Russo Gallery; Francine Seders Gallery; Arlene and Harold Schnitzer.

Partial operating support is provided to the Boise Art Museum by the City of Boise, the Idaho Commission on the Arts, and the National Endowment for the Arts, a Federal agency, Washington, D.C.

Boise Art Museum
670 South Julia Davis Drive
Boise, Idaho 83702
(208) 345-8330

Distributed by University
of Washington Press
P.O. Box 50096
Seattle, Washington 98145

Library of Congress
Cataloging-in-Publication Data

Harthorn, Sandy, 1945-
Fay Jones: a 20 year retrospective / organized by Sandy Harthorn; essays by Regina Hackett, Sondra Shulman.
p. cm.
Boise Art Museum, Boise, Idaho, August 31-October 27, 1996; Washington State University Museum of Art, Pullman, Washington, January 14-February 23, 1997; Seattle Art Museum, Seattle, Washington, March 20-July 22, 1997 —T.p. verso.
Includes bibliographical references.
1. Jones, Fay, 1936- —Exhibitions. I. Hackett, Regina, 1947- II. Shulman, Sondra, 1932- III. Boise Art Museum. IV. Washington State University. Museum of Art. V. Seattle Art Museum. VI. Title.
N6537.J668A4 1996 96-28667
709'.2—dc20
CIP

Cover: ***Self Portrait: Braque Boxing,*** 1992
acrylic on paper, 77" x 53-1/2"
Boise Art Museum Permanent Collection, Collectors Forum Purchase

Sponsors of the Exhibition

Stoel Rives LLP, Attorneys
Boise, Idaho
Seattle, Washington

Montgomery Watson Americas, Inc., Engineers
Boise, Idaho
Portland, Oregon
Bellevue, Washington

Grover/Thurston Gallery
Seattle, Washington

Laura Russo Gallery
Portland, Oregon

Francine Seders Gallery
Seattle, Washington

Arlene and Harold Schnitzer
Portland, Oregon

Lenders to the Exhibition

Donna Benaroya
Jill and Jay Bernstein
Sonja Blomdahl and Dick Weiss
Dianne Elliott
Hattie and Davis Freeman
Ann Gardner and Mitchell Karton
Jon Gierlich
Douglas and Lila Goodman
Isabel Sim Hamilton and Charles S. Hamilton
Juliana and Paul Heyne
Dave Hornor and Patti Jones
Timothy F. and Susan M. Jones
Ronald and Carol Margolis
Markovitz/Millett
Gary and Mary Molyneaux
Deborah and Kenneth Novack
Laurie and Scott Oki
Daniel F. Robinson
Paul Schneider and Lauren Eulau
Arlene and Harold Schnitzer
Joel Schumacher
Francine Seders
Sondra and Robert Shulman
J and J Wagonfeld
Private Collections

Cheney Cowles Museum, Spokane, Washington
Grover/Thurston Gallery, Seattle, Washington
Jo Bar & Rotisserie, Portland, Oregon
Laura Russo Gallery, Portland, Oregon
Microsoft Corporation, Redmond, Washington
Nishino, Seattle, Washington
Seattle City Light 1% for Art Portable Works Collection
and the Seattle Center Opera House
Shoshana Wayne Gallery, Santa Monica, California
Stoel Rives LLP, Attorneys, Seattle, Washington
Tacoma Art Museum, Tacoma, Washington

Foreword

The presentation of this significant retrospective exhibition by Fay Jones is both a momentous occasion as well as a stunning accomplishment. Fay Jones is an artist of considerable reputation in the Northwest and the Museum is fortunate and grateful to have this opportunity to display a broad range of her art to a wide regional audience.

The exhibition and its accompanying catalog with two insightful essays by Northwest writers Regina Hackett and Sondra Shulman provide the audience with a fresh perspective and understanding of Fay Jones' art. The publication also serves the purpose of exposing her art far beyond the region, where it will become better known and appreciated.

Fay Jones' enthusiastic willingness to participate in the project and her assistance throughout have made the process an exhilarating experience. I wish to recognize Sandy Harthorn, the Museum's Curator of Exhibitions, whose commitment to Northwest artists is well known. She had the vision to initiate the project and has skillfully fulfilled the complex enterprise of assembling this important retrospective of Fay Jones' artistic career, as well as providing an informative Introduction for this catalog. The Museum's curatorial staff has admirably responded to the total effort, bringing the innumerable aspects of the project to fruition.

Sandy graciously acknowledges the Museum's gratitude to all those who helped with the preparation of the exhibition and catalog in her Introduction. I would be remiss, however, if I did not credit our sponsors, whose contributions not only made this project possible, but provided the means to fully realize our vision. Stoel Rives Attorneys' major contribution made the difference in the scope and scale of this publication; Montgomery Watson Engineers, Grover/Thurston Gallery, and Laura Russo Gallery each made important leadership gifts; and Francine Seders Gallery and Arlene and Harold Schnitzer also made significant donations. We are indebted to them for their belief in this project and affection for the work of Fay Jones.

The Museum of Art at Washington State University, Pullman, and the Seattle Art Museum are also important contributors to the success of the Fay Jones retrospective exhibition. Their commitment to participate in the tour ensures a wide regional audience for the exhibition. We are pleased to be in partnership with these two fine museums.

The presentation of exhibitions by major and emerging Northwest artists, accompanied by significant publications, is a primary objective of the Boise Art Museum. I am continually gratified by the knowledge that the Museum staff is dedicated to this challenge. The Board of Trustees understands and encourages the professional responsibilities of the institution and plays an important role in these accomplishments. All of us who have worked on *Fay Jones: A 20 Year Retrospective* have gained new insights and respect for the artist's achievements. The Boise Art Museum is extremely proud to present this exhibition celebrating the art of Fay Jones.

Dennis O'Leary
Executive Director

Introduction

While preparing for this retrospective exhibition I had the pleasure of interviewing Fay Jones at her home on Seattle's north side, where we spent an evening discussing her art. We sat at her dining room table and as Fay spoke, I found that visually she could have stepped from one of her paintings. A backdrop of mint green doors and walls the color of pomegranate framed her expressive gestures and billowing hair. I remember it so clearly because like her paintings, Fay Jones describes her experiences in vivid terms. As she spoke of her family, her background and artwork, her words created an outpouring of stories interspersed with personal wisdom and perceptive insights. It quickly became evident how much Fay's heritage, circumstances, and the incidents of her daily life directly influence her work.

When Fay Jones speaks of her family, her eyes glisten. The eldest of six, Jones grew up in a household which she describes as "well versed in chaos." The equilibrium of homelife was compromised by the fact that her parents owned and operated a hotel, restaurant and bar, and as a young woman, it was her responsibility to maintain order for the younger siblings. Fay considers the escapades of the quirky hotel family in John Irving's novel *Hotel New Hampshire* as being somewhat reminiscent of her own. Jones' impressions of her atypical family life laid the groundwork for imagery that later surfaces in her art.

Jones decided at an early age to become an artist, and entered the Rhode Island School of Design at seventeen. She met her husband, painter Robert Jones, at the school, graduated at twenty and had four children before she was thirty. When her husband was appointed to a teaching position at the University of Washington Art Department in 1960, their family moved to Seattle. As Jones' children grew older and departed, she converted the living room into a studio and began painting in earnest.

Jones readily acknowledges that her images are semi-autobiographical; they are not literal, yet they hold an essence of truth. For example, references to the sea, pools, and water reoccur in numerous paintings. Jones, who has always lived by water, finds both romance and danger connected to images of the sea. She explains that her ancestors include seafaring people and that she is instinctively drawn to places near water. Conversely, the artist nearly drowned as a child, and water has since symbolized an element to be overcome.

Jones takes full advantage of the use of personal symbols as a means to express emotions on paper. Unpredictably, Jones inserts palm trees, fish, houses, clocks, sailors, boxing gloves and other details in her compositions. These images represent ideas about far off places, nourishment, domesticity, history, romance and marriage. It is a language, once recognized, that gives you a key to the work.

The paintings and mixed-media collages selected for this retrospective exhibition survey four main periods in the artist's career. From the early 1970s to 1977, Jones' works were primarily diaristic. The artist created figural compositions in outdoor settings that explored her reflections on social conventions and interpersonal relationships.

From 1977 to 1980, Jones became a socially conscious observer, moving beyond the personal views of a diarist. Her paintings

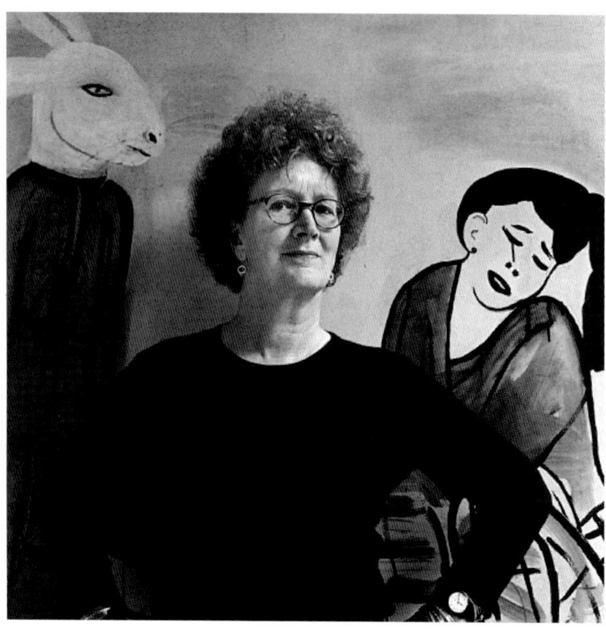

Artist Fay Jones

grew in scale, while background landscapes and vestiges of atmospheric perspective were eliminated from the compositions. The figures became more prominent, assuming greater than life-size proportions.

During the 1980s Jones developed contrived fictions of painted stage sets in which all real space disappears and the artist incorporates theatrical devices. Figural gestures in the paintings are those of actors or mimes; there is a distillation of events or activities, and reoccurring symbols function as props. Diverse and conflicting figures lay one upon the other, overlapping like cutouts or paper dolls. Rendered in a geometric framework, they gain a sense of monumentality and take on the rhetoric of the stage. Jones talks about her eyesight playing a role in this imagery: "I have flat vision." This way of seeing opens up unique possibilities for juxtaposing characters, resulting in a style that has become a signature for the artist.

Along with her visual approach, Jones believes that the power of words to evoke images is equally important. The artist creates with the spirit of a writer and conceives her painted figures as if they are fictional characters developed in an author's imagination. Inspired by writers such as Marcel Proust, Emily Bronte, Jack Kerouac, John Updike and Betty Friedan among others, she composes a visual poetry to portray complicated emotions and associations.

In 1984, Jones was awarded an Individual Artist Fellowship Grant from Washington State Arts Commission to make a series of twelve paired book collages that are both autobiographical and about her own reading history. From this period onward, Fay Jones increasingly uses literary sources, such as Lewis Carroll's *Alice in Wonderland* and Sam Shepard's *Motel*

Chronicles, as the basis for narratives of caustic commentary that are meant to question values and assumptions. In these, as in recent works, Jones demonstrates her innate ability to suggest dynamics between her characters through the nuances of looks and gestures.

During the 1990s, Jones has incorporated a lighter, brighter palette and a bolder rendering of shapes; she has found elegance in the simplification of forms and a directness that is poised and assured. In the framework of her paintings, Fay Jones has chronicled her lifetime of impressions, observations, and reflections, all peppered with brilliant imagination and wry humor. What we are drawn to in the magnetic appeal of Fay Jones' art is her understanding of the mysterious nature of relationships and the complexity of human emotions.

The forty-three paintings, drawings and mixed-media works included in this exhibition have been selected from public and private collections in Boise, Seattle, Tacoma, Spokane, Portland, Los Angeles, and New York. I wish to acknowledge with special thanks all of the collectors and lenders who are passionate about living with Fay Jones' art and who have agreed to lend their works for an extended period to this exhibition and tour. We greatly appreciate the thirty-seven collectors, corporations and museums who have given their support by contributing works for this exhibition.

Our sincere gratitude is also extended to the sponsors, without whose commitment this exhibition, catalog and tour could not take place. We are indebted to Stoel Rives LLP, Attorneys, Boise and Seattle; Montgomery Watson Americas, Inc., Engineers, Boise, Portland, and Bellevue; Grover/Thurston Gallery, Seattle; Laura Russo Gallery, Portland; Francine Seders Gallery, Seattle; and Arlene and Harold Schnitzer for their generous contributions to this retrospective exhibition and its accompanying catalog.

Special thanks go to Susan Grover and Richard Thurston, Fay Jones' gallery representatives in Seattle, for their invaluable assistance in providing materials and coordinating loans. Laura Russo, who represents Jones in Portland, was equally supportive with loans from that area.

We are indebted to Patricia Watkinson, Director, Washington State University Museum of Art, and Vicki Halper, Associate Curator of Modern Art, Seattle Art Museum, who have enthusiastically supported the presentation of this exhibition from its inception. Their participation is a testament to the admiration they have for Fay Jones' work.

We are grateful to writers Regina Hackett and Sondra Shulman for sharing their insights and literary skills. Their essays offer a sensitive and reflective view of Fay Jones' oeuvre. As always, I greatly appreciate the staff of the Boise Art Museum for their support, most especially Dennis O'Leary for his complete confidence in Fay Jones and the exhibition; and Cynthia Sewell and Kathleen Bettis for their editorial skills, patience and devotion to the project.

Throughout every phase of the exhibition Fay Jones has been a superlative participant in every way – always generous, eager to assist and completely dedicated. We cherish Fay Jones for her talent and gracious personality and thank her wholeheartedly for painting fabulous fictions brimming with spirit and soul.

Sandy Harthorn, Curator of Exhibitions

Fay Jones: Inner Landscapes
Sondra Shulman

On the corner of First Avenue and Madison below the city's skyline but above the rush of Seattle traffic you could once see a flock of geese streaking through a blue sky full of white, puffy, pink-tinged clouds. These were not ordinary birds. Silent instead of noisy, defying weather and season, oblivious to the clatter of horns, the glare of stop lights and the stench of diesel, some with ornately patterned wings, some of them nothing but their own silhouettes or shadow, flying both in and out of formation, they pursued a steady west-east course as if on a backwards journey across the continent, a journey that would carry them through time as well as space.

The brick wall over Warshal's Sporting Goods has since been painted over. The geese that Fay Jones sent soaring into the blue are long gone. They and their short-lived flight are reminders of the fragility of art. That I still see them whenever I pass the spot where they used to be, that they are etched in my memory, is a tribute to the power of Fay Jones' skill and imagination.

But if the birds are gone, the landscapes they flew over remain and reappear in a dozen different ways. They are landscapes of the mind, honest and uncompromising and as American as a Fourth of July picnic, the daily newspaper, a prize fight or a fishing hole. They span the last half of the twentieth century but reach back into time just as they reach forwards, absorbing both past and future into an always changing and open-ended present. Like skew mirrors they depict who we are, the culture we have grown out of and a world in flux where nothing is predetermined.

Fay Jones' paintings spur our collective psyches. But they are more than conscious renderings of the unconscious. In viewing them, we enter a universe in which reality masquerades as dream, life is as unpredictable as it is ominous, and where everyday, ordinary rhythms are heightened by the blare of the preposterous. We live in a century which has gone from Kitty Hawk to the moon walk and beyond, where gender is ambiguous and where cyberspace can eliminate in a second the four thousand miles between Toledo, Ohio, and Toledo, Spain. Should we really be surprised we can no longer find refuge in the routine or be startled when a goose stares out the second story window of a moon-stenciled pink house, or that a stilt man is taller than the buildings he walks in front of; that a fish, a red one to boot, is bigger than the pond he lives in or, as in *Body Fires* (page 44), it is impossible for the three figures to keep their inner feelings hidden and what we see are the blazes that ultimately might consume them?

These images and others like them – a stone boat with a skimpy blue sail and a tilted candlestick on its bow, a woman with a lotus pod on her head, a coliseum-like structure rising out of the sea – throw us off keel. We hold on to them the way we would the planks of a boat in which we have been overturned only to find out that whether we have wanted to or not we have sunk beyond our depths. This of course is Fay Jones' genius – her diabolical ability to pull us in. Her wizardry is unlimited. We see it as much in the way she paints – the stenciled ironies, the unforced juxtapositions – as in what she paints. In *Salmon Man* (page 16), artist and sorcerer, though not completely interchangeable, have the same primal concerns. Life and death are at the center of the picture as they are of our beings.

If there is sleight of hand, it is that as viewers we come away unsure of the cosmic trick that has been played on us and discover that the real magician is a force over which we have absolutely no control. We are born and we die and the in-between is a blank canvas we may or may not know how to fill. Often the panorama that emerges has as much to do with others as ourselves and, paradoxically, some of these others might be ourselves. As a painter, Fay Jones depicts our inner and outer makeup, the faces we show, the faces we keep hidden or mask. She sees past our failures, confusions, and disappointments, our posturing and subterfuges, even past our dreams and minor triumphs to our basic natures. What she says to us through a fish-legged ballerina or a muscular, pipe-smoking woman armed with her butterfly net is that we are who we aren't as well as who we are. Like those self-absorbed lovers in *Sheet Music* (page 42) our sins are those of avoidance and apathy. If we are satisfied with ourselves we have nothing further to do than go on to the next picture. That we aren't and that we don't, that we try to resolve the complexities of both painting and self, is the result of the dialogue the artist has engaged us in. Soon we begin to make up our own stories.

History might be a clock perched on a locked chest; marriage, a pair of black boxing gloves or two red rabbits dancing; our unformed intellects and instincts, Buddha babies; being and the end of being, two amorphous pools around which is scattered the litter – animal, vegetable and mineral – of our lives.

Whatever leaps our minds take, whatever interpretations we give to or conclusions we draw from these paintings, we never depart too far from their puzzling truths, and in scenes unmediated by convention or contained by certainty we test our own limits and question our views, values and assumptions. In viewing Fay Jones we travel through seemingly chaotic terrains where we find ordinary expectations upended, time illusory and existence as tenuous and as changeful as the black ripples on an orange-blue pond. Along the way we encounter a fiery-haired jester, an angel-winged picnicker, horses at a language lesson, dogs cavorting in a patch of flesh-pink sky – the list goes on and on – all anarchic, all subverting a preconceived reality.

The stories we have told ourselves merge with and emerge from the stories in the paintings. They are obscure, mysterious, unpredictable and not easy to decode. We soon realize meaning is itself an anomaly and that there is no Rosetta stone for matters of spirit and mind. And yet we want to understand.

We follow spaces, shapes, strokes, colors. We pay attention to the small patterns and the larger schemes. We make note of a red diving board, a red shirt collar, a red sailor suit, a woman lying on the beach whose hair, skin and clothes are also red and we attempt to connect one to the other as if their color were the key to their core. We do this because we are dealing with a complex and formidable body of work. Fay Jones' paintings are as serious and wise as they are witty and ironic. In a world where the cataclysmic seems to be the norm they point out the failure of institutions, traditions and rituals to halt further havoc. Against this setting we quickly find out we are not alone in our fears and apprehensions and that those uncanny sailors and wily magicians in all their many guises and disguises cannot help us anymore than they can help themselves. In *Mistral* (page 38) we are subtly shown the dilemma that faces us – a door, slightly ajar, that leads from the sea to a whirlwind. What amazes us is how much joy we take in confronting the profound.

Fay Jones as artist reaches into those secret places we have left unguarded. We are made to feel. And though we cannot always articulate our emotions we might say we know, as in *Woman Weeping Pears* (page 43), what it's like to have our dreams weighted down and our desires turned into tears.

In the end these paintings change the way we view ourselves and the world we live in. Like those disappeared geese, they become part of the landscape of our own minds. What more can we ask of art?

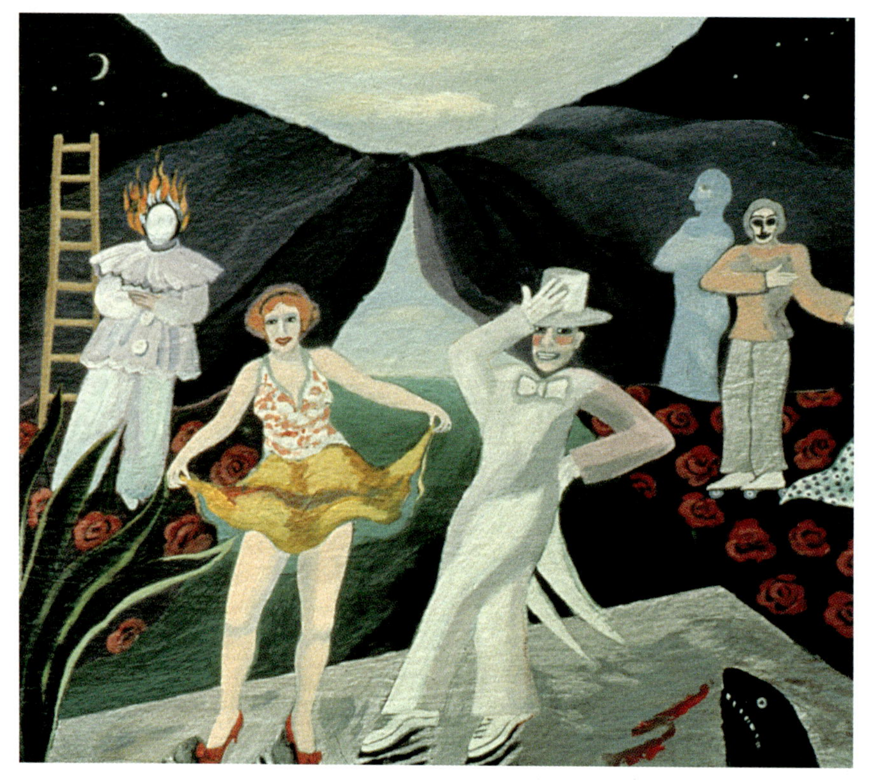

Dance on Thin Ice, 1975
acrylic on paper
10" x 11"
Collection of Dave Hornor and Patti Jones

Fay Jones And The Amorous Realm
Regina Hackett

In the amorous realm, the most painful wounds are inflicted more often by what one sees than by what one knows.
Roland Barthes, *A Lover's Discourse*

Winter is over, but the man and woman skating on thin ice fail to notice. As the ground beneath their bladed feet begins to give way, he tips his ghostly top hat, and she lifts her sour yellow skirt in invitation. Sunk in their private drama, they also fail to notice a cavity of sky cut into the dark. Pitched overhead like a transparent bowl of blue light, it overflows and allows a trickle of new weather to spill into their cave, signaling the end of their alliance.

With *Dance on Thin Ice* (facing page), Seattle's Fay Jones was toying with her central theme: the limits of allure. She has always been drawn to the male/female conjunction and uses painting to explore the outer edge of its desires. Romance in her hands becomes memory. She paints it alive in the world and allows it to color land, sky and everything between.

As is usual with Jones, the stark clarity of *Dance on Thin Ice* conceals its thematic complications. Here is a passion fueled by chill, not heat. The male has a dandy's elegance. His body could have been modeled on an Elie Nadelman sculpture, but his face is pure James Ensor. It's both mask and flesh, utterly unreachable behind its good manners. The woman is human. Hopes high and stomach sucked in, she lifts her dress over her pudgy white thighs and smiles in futile invitation. The viewer knows what she does not, that she will never secure him. She is exposing herself to no useful end. The ground that will momentarily give way beneath her will continue to hold him up. He is an illusion and therefore free to move on.

If the dead white of her legs brings to mind the boy disappearing in Bruegel's *Icarus*, leaving only his legs to mark his presence in the painting, the confident course of Jones' heedless male resembles that of the ship that didn't check its course just because a boy fell to doom beside it.

Because it's an old story, Jones gave it a comic edge to undermine its tragic glamour. The night that is parting to admit the day's blue is only a stage curtain. As it gives way, so do the night's revels. Drawn on the curtain are dark blue highways to nowhere, mountainous pillows that offer no rest and the illusory emblems of starry romance: bright planets and the curved, sideways smile of the quarter moon. The skating rink is a stage, and the figures on it actors. As they move to their drama's conclusion, a trio of other actors stands around, bored in advance by the inevitable.

Dance on Thin Ice is striking for both its strengths and weaknesses. Like a jack sprung to life while still inside its box, the painting seems unhappily compressed into the small space allowed it. Its colors are fierce but choked, its figures stiff instead of seductive. *Dance on Thin Ice* has the charms – and limitations – of a folk miniature. If Jones had stopped painting at this point, roughly twenty years after graduating from the Rhode Island School of Design in Providence, R.I., and fifteen years after moving to Seattle, she'd be remembered in the Northwest as an eccentric visual aphorist whose densities and complications could amaze and sometimes frustrate her audience.

Fortunately, as this retrospective organized by Sandy Harthorn of the Boise Art Museum makes clear, Jones went on to open her previously constricted spaces and set her figures free. By the early 1980s, in her mid-forties, her colors began to bloom with a lush, glowing intensity that is rare in acrylics. During this crucial period, her confidence increased with her dimensions. She began painting with her whole arm instead of just her hand, making spaces through which her figures could move and breathe.

With new possibilities for motion, her figures changed their character. Instead of stalwart and stocky, they became sleek and elusive. Filled with air and colored light, they acquired serious glamour. Like heroes and heroines discovered at the end of the play to be of noble blood, Jones' figures discovered new relations. They began to resemble the high-fashion, fortunate few constructed by Alex Katz.

The connection is real but superficial. Unlike Jones, Katz paints in the classical mode. His mood is physical, frank and extroverted. There's nothing classical about Jones. Her work is spiritual instead of physical, mysterious instead of frank, introverted instead of extroverted. These attributes make her sound almost medieval, and yet she paints large and light, with a feeling of powder, perfume and artifice.

No artist can be reduced to her sources, but a measure of Jones' originality can be taken from what she has borrowed. The elegance of her simplifications owes something to Katz, but the glorious radiance of her color, her fascination with the "fête galante" or feast of courtship, comes from an earlier era. Jones has created a contemporary version of eighteenth-century pleasure painting, Antoine Watteau's in particular. She shares his interest in colored air and theatrics, in flirtations and fallings out. Like him, she offers no obvious plot or resolution of events but manages to suggest the amplitude of a full narrative.

Jones came into her own in the 1980s and found herself noticed as never before. As curator Bruce Guenther pointed out in a catalog essay for a 1985 exhibit at the Seattle Art Museum, Jones at this time had the unexpected pleasure of finding herself in step with the art world.

With her precise miniatures, she had rejected the abstract expressionism dominant in her youth, and she sailed through thc 1960s and 1970s without acknowledging the influences of latter-day Pop, minimalism or geometric abstraction. But in the 1980s, new artists provoked an interest in new forms of expressive painting with narrative imagery, and Jones' reputation began its upward soar.

Narrative imagery is Jones' forte. Her acrylics on paper are meant to be read. They are paintings whose volumes and atmospheres imply a text, a form of speech whose meanings are coded into visual sensations and intuitions. And even when these texts overlap and need to be read simultaneously, they are notable for their dream-time clarity. Underlying their dreaminess is a complex network of formal relationships: orchestrated colors that work with planes, curves and angles to echo and affirm each other.

Bird Cage (page 22) from 1981 is a tribute to Max Beckmann's nightmarish triptych, *Departure,* from 1932-33. She brings his abstracted tortures into her personal, poetic realm without taming them. *Bird Cage* is a world of missed connections, unified by a subtle range of exclusively primary colors and an underlying network of structural elements. The swell of hip echoes the curve of a duck's neck, and fingers spread like the roots of a distant tree.

At this point, Jones became able to give even her smaller works a sense of expanded scale. In 1985 she developed a series of collages – paint over pages of book text, pasted randomly and at angles across her painting's space. Using text as ground for painting is an idea she developed about the same time as did Tim Rollins and K.O.S. (Kids of Survival), she without knowledge of them.

Her version is less abstract and more painterly. In acrylic she drew a spare grouping of figures and occasionally the edges of clouds on top of book texts. These are her Alice paintings, from *Alice in Wonderland* (pages 26, 27). In one, Alice is outlined in black, wearing her famous white apron and ready for croquet, holding a flamingo to use as a stick, the body of each filled with print. The young girl gamely masters the enlarged male symbol, putting it, as did her fictional forbear, to absurdist use.

In another, Alice has lost her way. She stands like Hester Prynne on the scaffold or like Jane Eyre disgraced at school as a liar, her face blanked out. Below, a refugee from an Edward Hopper painting (the usher leaning against a wall in an old theater) comes to Alice's rescue, enlivened by feminist concern. Wearing boxing gloves and dominating the still visible shadow of her formerly passive self, she shouts at Alice to abandon the pedestal of her disgrace.

Lovers perform lunatic chores. Wrapped as a bald baby Buddha, the lover in *Language Lesson* (page 36) feeds herself on dreams, ignoring the snide commentary of a trio of white horse heads, in profile to her left. Jones has a freewheeling, new freedom here, a casual, conjuring grace that allows her to improvise with materials in the same dexterous way she had always improvised with meaning. Increasingly, as in *Language Lesson*, she shuffles and plays new cards from her image deck, including collaged bits of Chinese gift paper, pasted on the surface like extra postage for rapid delivery.

Her tragedies are not often allowed to take themselves seriously. The dogs of the street will eat Jezebel, warn the queens of tragedy, schooled on society's strictures and holding hands up to their ashed faces in disapproval (*Tragic and Comedic Queens*, page 25). Don't say that unless you're willing to do some barking, replies Jones' ribald queen, bracketed by her shocked sisters. The Jezebel happily ignoring dire alarms is dressed in tight red. A train track opens behind her and a blurred blue bunny, the symbol of wanton fecundity, is poised mid-run over her left shoulder.

Can women die from being dumped? Only from buildings. The heroine of *Demi-Mondaine* (page 35) is a world entire. Flowers fall across the swell of her hips, and her linebacker's powerful arms are folded under her powdery blue breasts. She is an axis on which the painting turns. Lesser mortals, half her size, ricochet around her, the dream debris of her life. A featherless biped, plucked and pimply, stands behind her, the dashed male. Someone in a rowboat makes a hasty retreat.

Hats fly and flowers open in the richly colored air around her. The painting could be a record of where she has been, the past she is amply able to surmount.

It could also be the dream of the anguished lover, the sailor in red on the left, romanticizing his losses. She could be, as Roland Barthes noted in *A Lover's Discourse*, the "paltry character of a powerful, tormented, flamboyant drama staged by the subject....placed in the center of the stage and there adored, idolized, taken to task, covered with discourse, with prayers (and perhaps, surreptitiously, with invective), as if she were a huge, motionless hen huddled amid her feathers, around which circles a slightly mad cock."

Jones' story lines are deliberately open, yet occasionally they converge. The giant woman in *Mistral* (page 38) is not the center of anyone's stage, even her own. She has disappeared into her mental weather. She's transparent, the features of her face in profile lined with blue, an echo of the blue man saluting beyond her from a boat. The home she is too large and loose to return to is threatened by the weight of her dark longing. Its black funnel appears behind her, but she, turned away, ignores its meaning, lost in faces she has known and landscapes in which she was once happy. The painting is ashy and pale, lit along its nerve endings by fragments of brighter, bolder tonalities.

Sailors are a constant for Jones, men who are only temporarily on land. The sailor in *Body Fires* (page 44) dreams of satisfactions, warming the white of his belly with orange. Sleeping, he is an oversized, white parenthesis folded in on itself, taken through sleep and with his defenses down into the moist, blue/green realm of foggy wet plant life.

In the middle panel, an androgynous figure, dressed as a male, heats the table on which his/her hand rests. It's a stage trick given oracle importance. The curtain flaps behind, and over the figure's derby hat smothers a mess of gold, a hint of a halo. In the last panel, a woman is transported by a heady embrace. Babies/Buddhas float on lily pads above her, and four black birds bear witness, each resting on a green shoot or Cupid's arrow.

Jones is also fond of men in baseball caps, the cap being the sign of the forever young. It's Jones' version of Jung's archetype known as "Puer Aeternus," the bud that will not open into maturity. In *Gifts* (page 50), two figures face each other in profile, a man and a woman made by black paint on brown paper. The man in the baseball cap hangs his head, staring down at his hands, which have turned into large red anchors. The woman sympathizes and waves frilly handkerchiefs. He is dangerous dead weight; she is useless, comforting gesture.

The triptych *Touch and Go* (page 48) is an odd and tender painting. Greater and lesser figures float on a variety of planes, defying gravity. At such heights the air is thin. Jones seems to be painting on membrane instead of paper. These figures are phantoms, recently passed from bodies to souls, and their embraces – though eternal – are not to be trusted. While a pair of red rabbits dances and black tendrils in a Ming-blue vase trace a languorous path overhead, a lone sailor amid the couples holds his dismayed white head in his hands. He and a trio of isolate babies function as a dissonant chorus. They are simultaneously aghast, supplicating and indifferent to the binding ties around them. Few artists paint with such a light yet pointed touch, with such deft swerve-and-dodge skills. Jones can retrieve images hovering at the edges of consciousness and give them coherence without flattening them into plot.

Carnal bonds can be barriers. Back to back stand a couple in *Souvenir* (page 56), she noticing the electric current of their conjunction, he seemingly oblivious. Book in hand and hat on his head (sign of his readiness to depart), he reads with a golden bubble coming out of his mouth. That's the talk he'll take her down with.

Men can be said to be missing from Jones' paintings, even when they're there. They are ghosts, memories, distractions and victims of tunnel vision: long darks for women to whistle through.

And yet, if men are a kind of illusion, there is an illusion under that illusion. Both male and female characters are ultimately projections of the artist herself, and her large cast is a subtle kind of self-portrait. Her painting comes from her capacity to express the whole of her experience, ranging freely across the divide of sexual role and its accompanying attributes. That is why these paintings with such a strong polarity of male/female action nevertheless have something of the androgynous about them.

Art for her is visual speech. It's more slippery than words, more free to suggest, imply and allude, to strike out and circle back, keeping disparate, even contradictory meanings alive without confusion.

Her paintings are tableaus, and her tableaus are stories, yet they are also baited traps, poised to spring. One moves around them with care as well as pleasure.

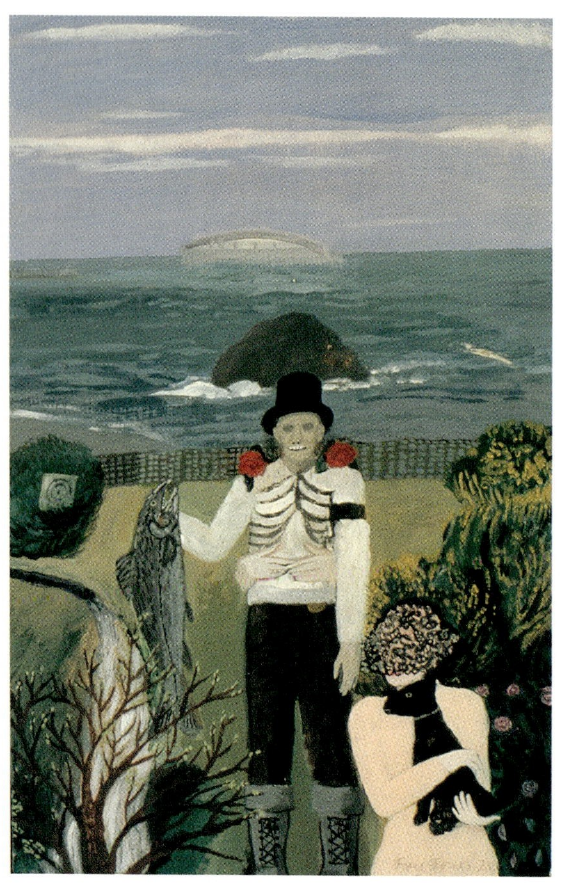

Salmon Man, 1973
acrylic on wood
11" x 7"
Collection of Jon Gierlich

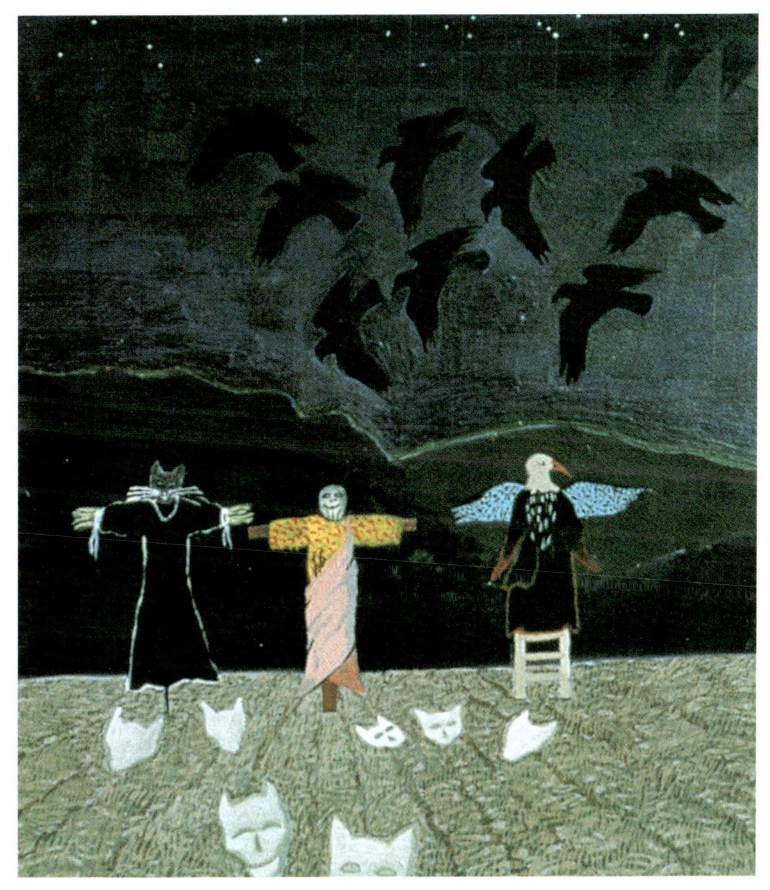

Crows, Scarecrows, 1974
acrylic and graphite on paper
10" x 9-1/8"
Collection of Francine Seders

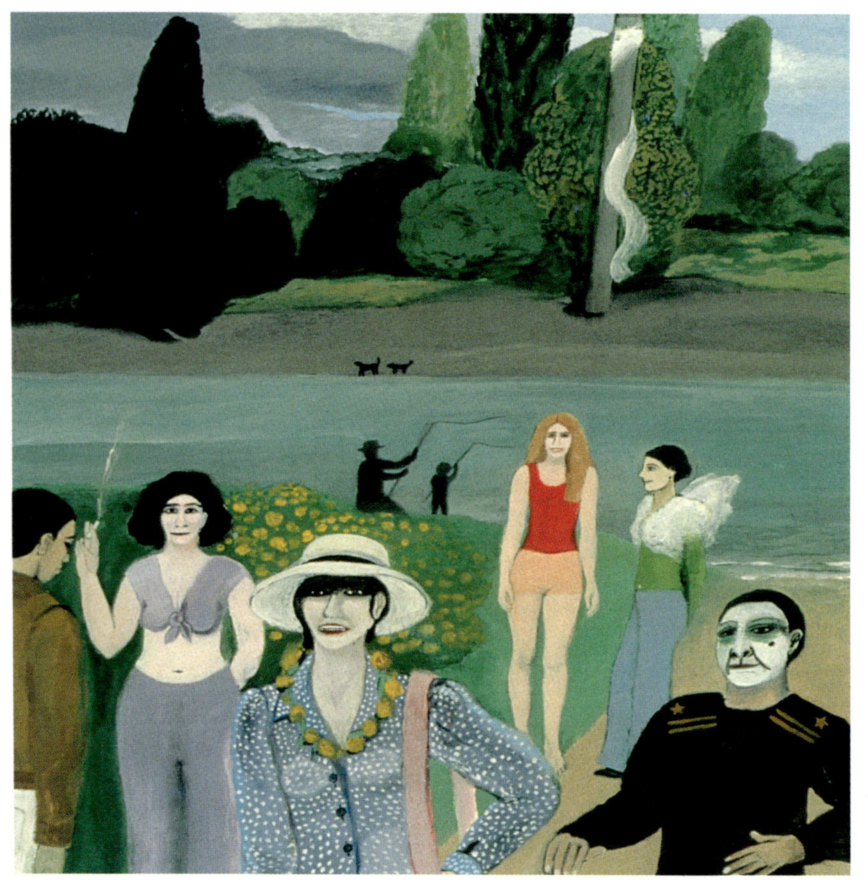

Picnic Spanning Three Seasons, 1974
acrylic on paper
20" x 17"
Collection of Sondra and Robert Shulman

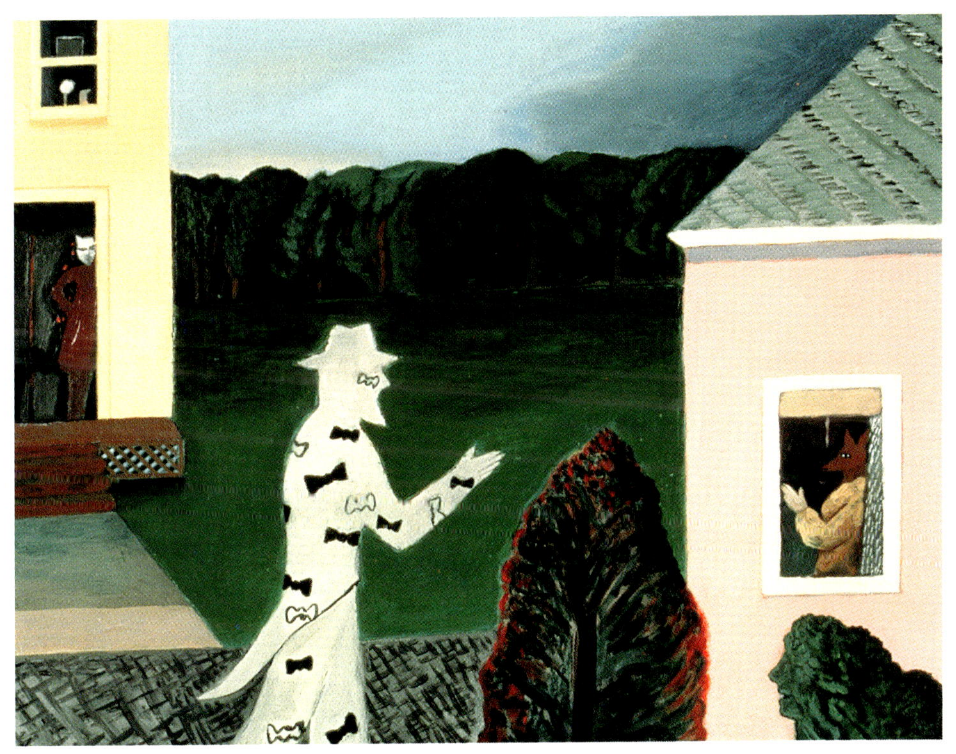

Nov. 22, 1976**,** 1978
acrylic on paper
15" x 20"
Collection of Juliana and Paul Heyne

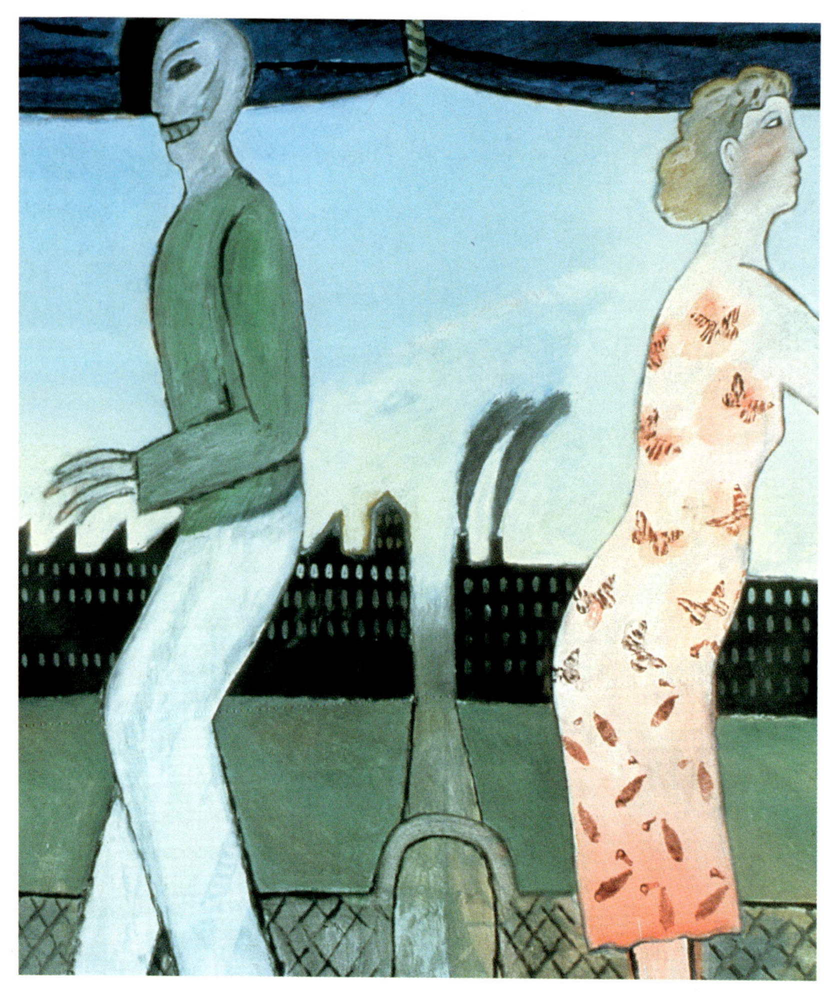

Past & Future Dos a Dos, 1980
acrylic on paper
53" x 47"
Collection of the artist

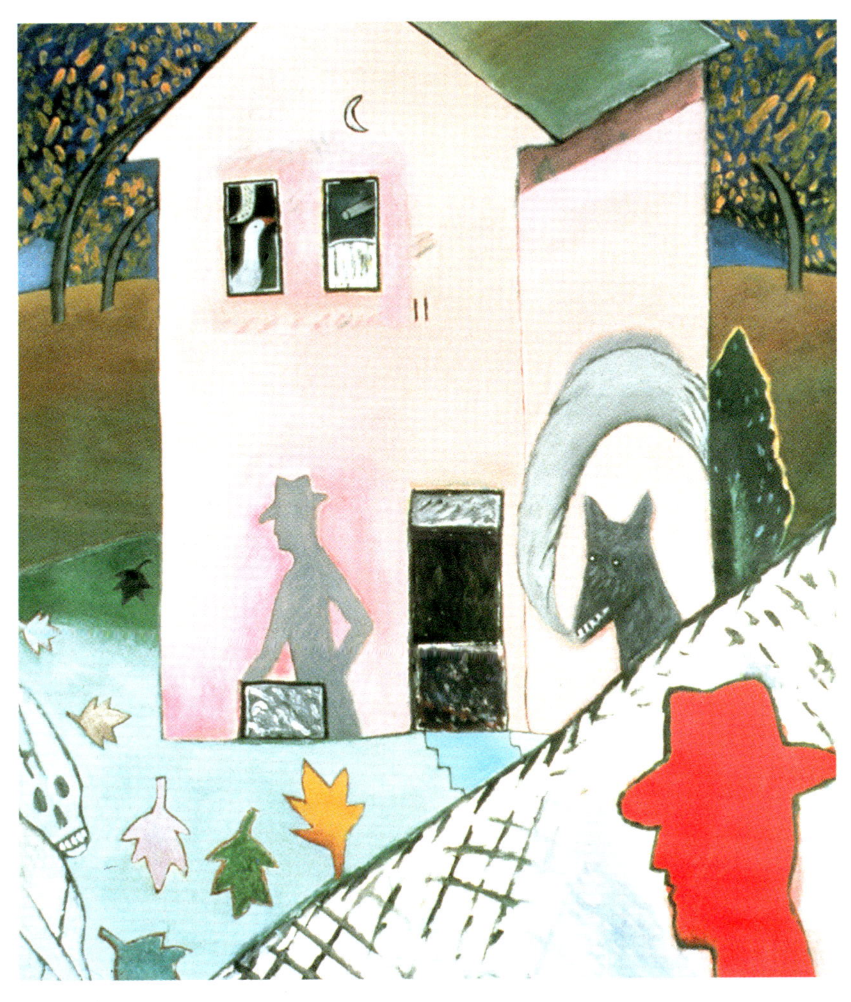

Pink House, Off Season, 1980
acrylic on paper
52-3/4" x 47-1/4"
Collection of Timothy F. and Susan M. Jones

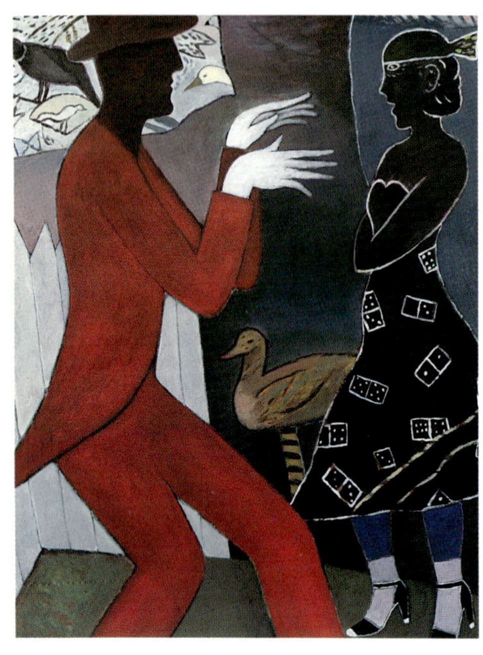

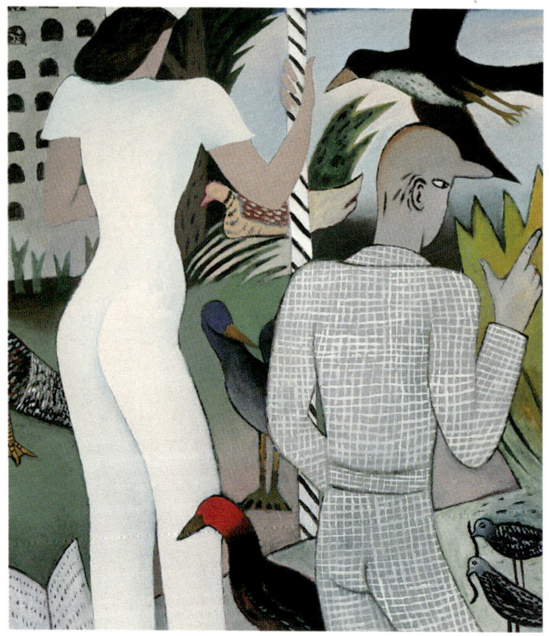

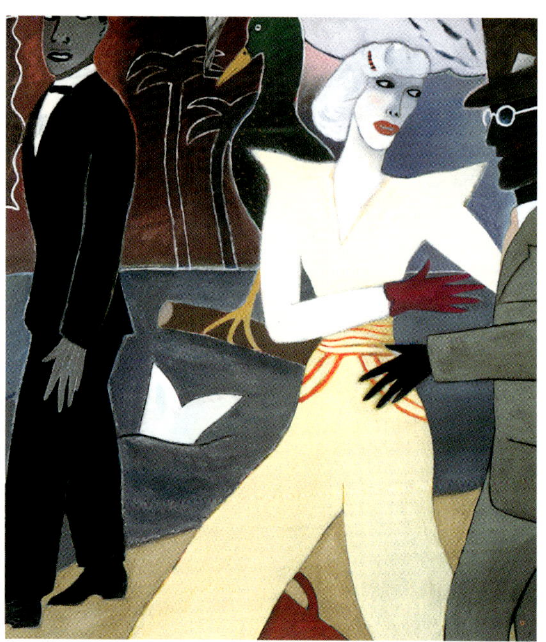

Bird Cage, 1981
acrylic on paper
triptych, 53" x 141"
Private Collection

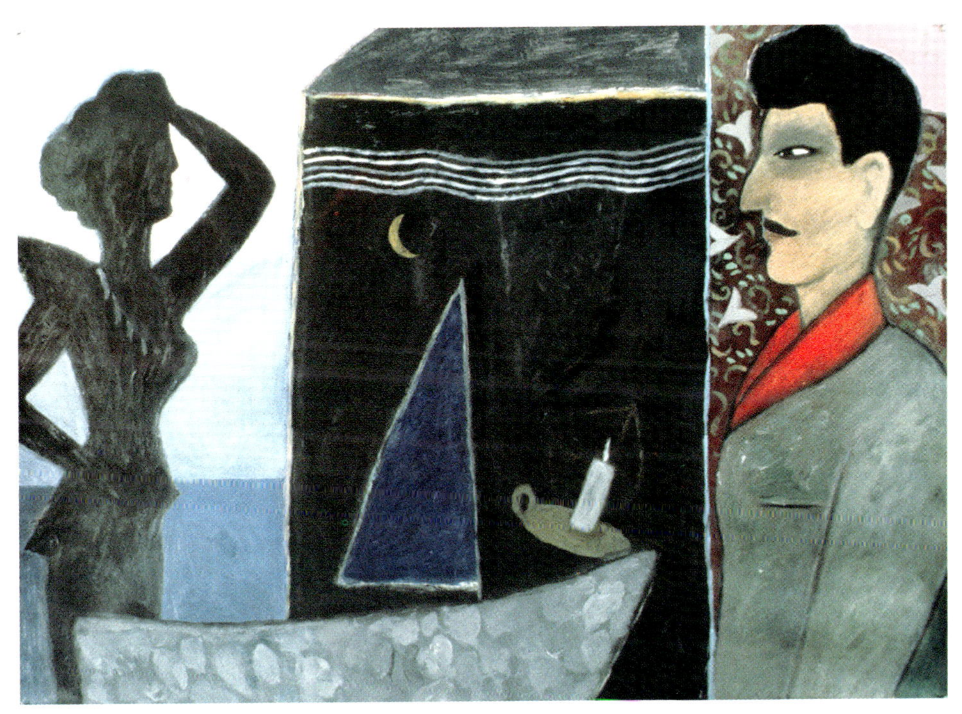

Rocco & the Stone Boat, 1983
acrylic on paper
27-1/2" x 39"
Collection of Hattie and Davis Freeman

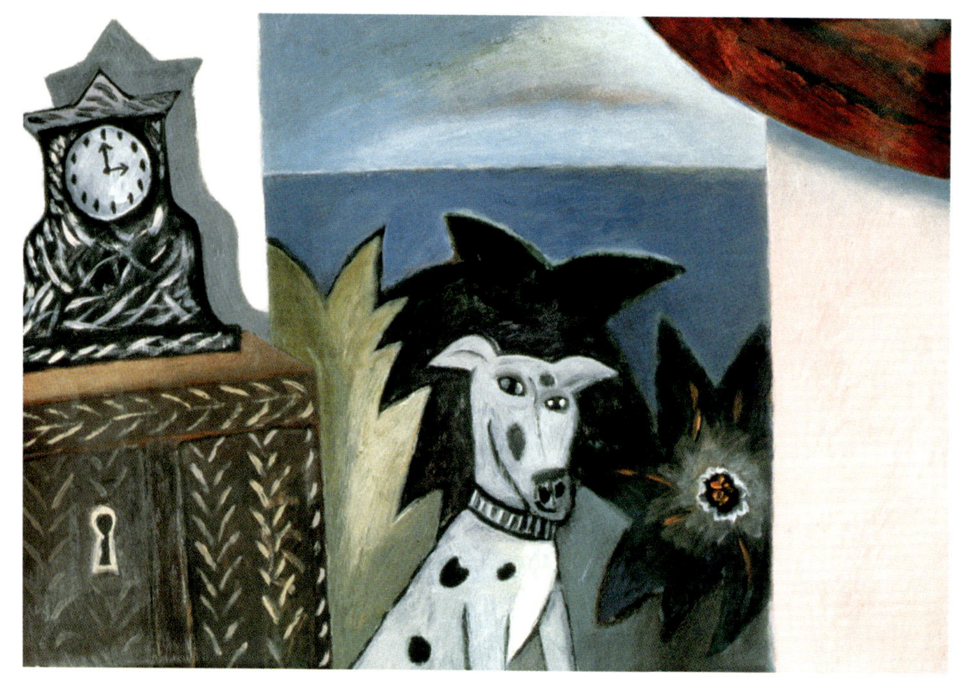

Siesta, Villa Carlotta, 1983
acrylic on paper
27-1/2" x 39"
Collection of Isabel Sim Hamilton and
Charles S. Hamilton

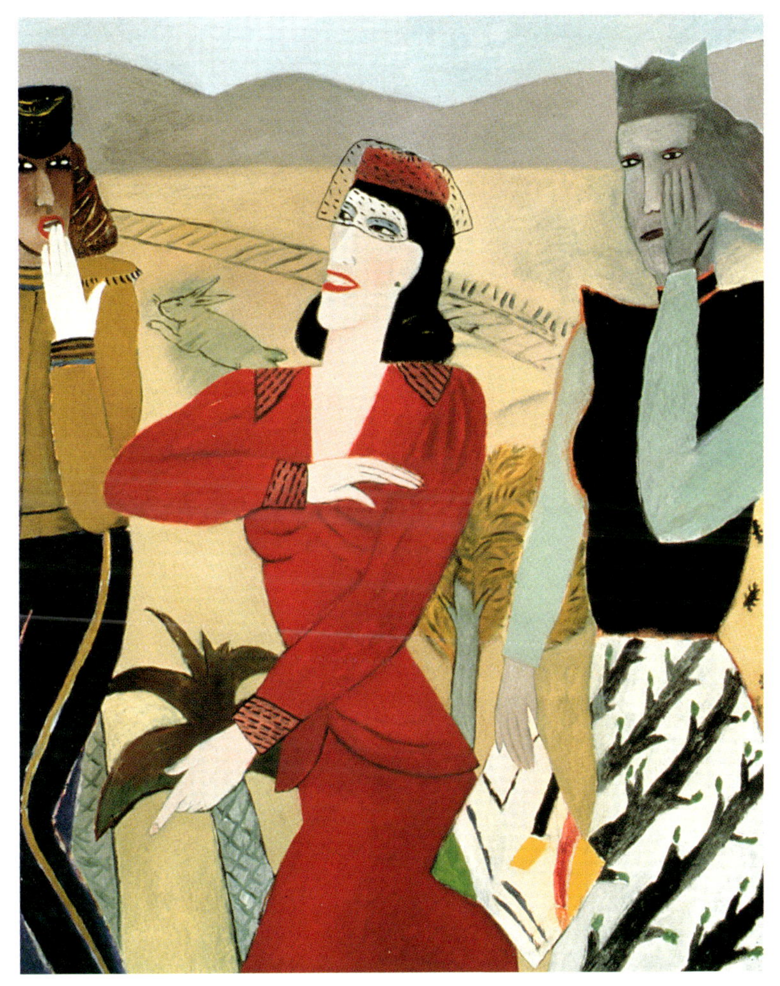

Tragic and Comedic Queens, 1984
acrylic on paper
66" x 52-1/2"
Collection of Joel Schumacher

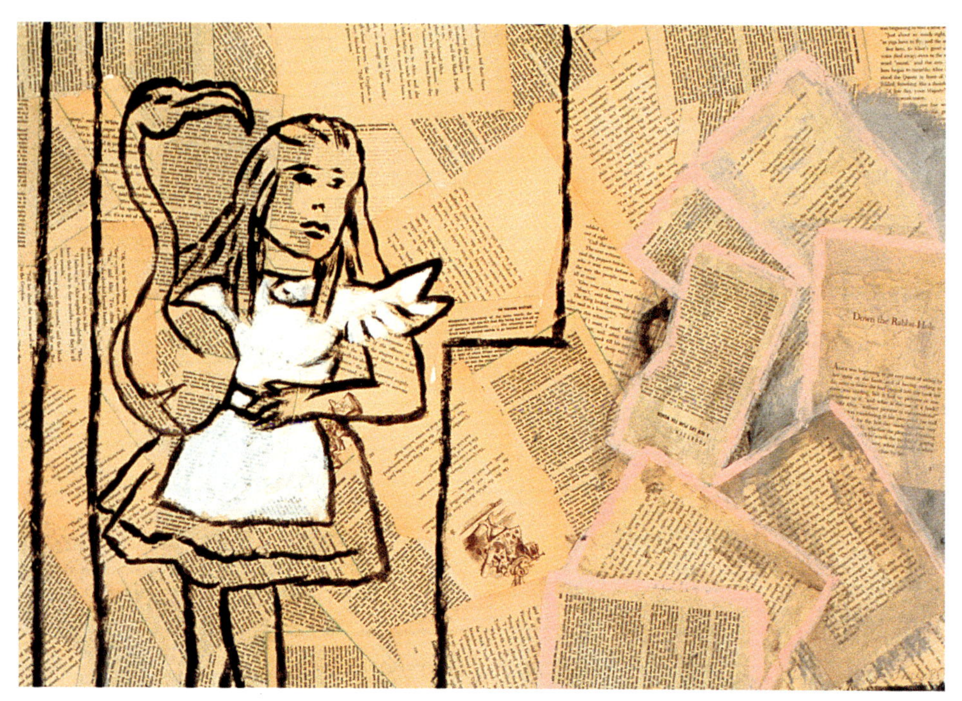

Alice Meets Betty, 1985
acrylic and collage on paper
27" x 39"
Collection of Markovitz/Millett

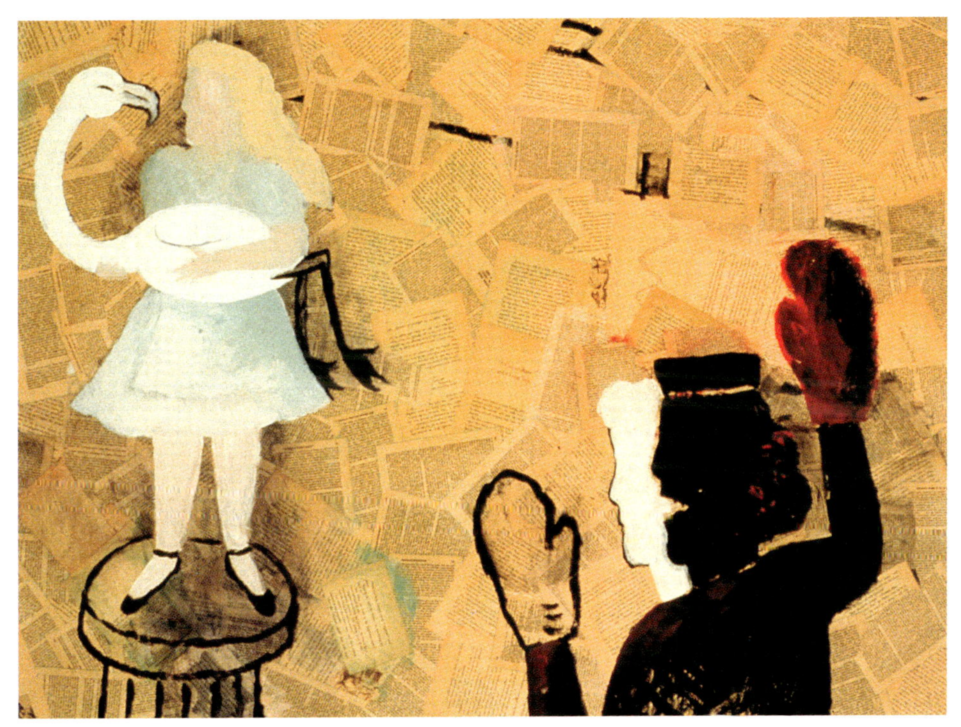

Alice vs. Betty, 1985
acrylic and collage on paper
39" x 53"
Collection of Sonja Blomdahl and Dick Weiss

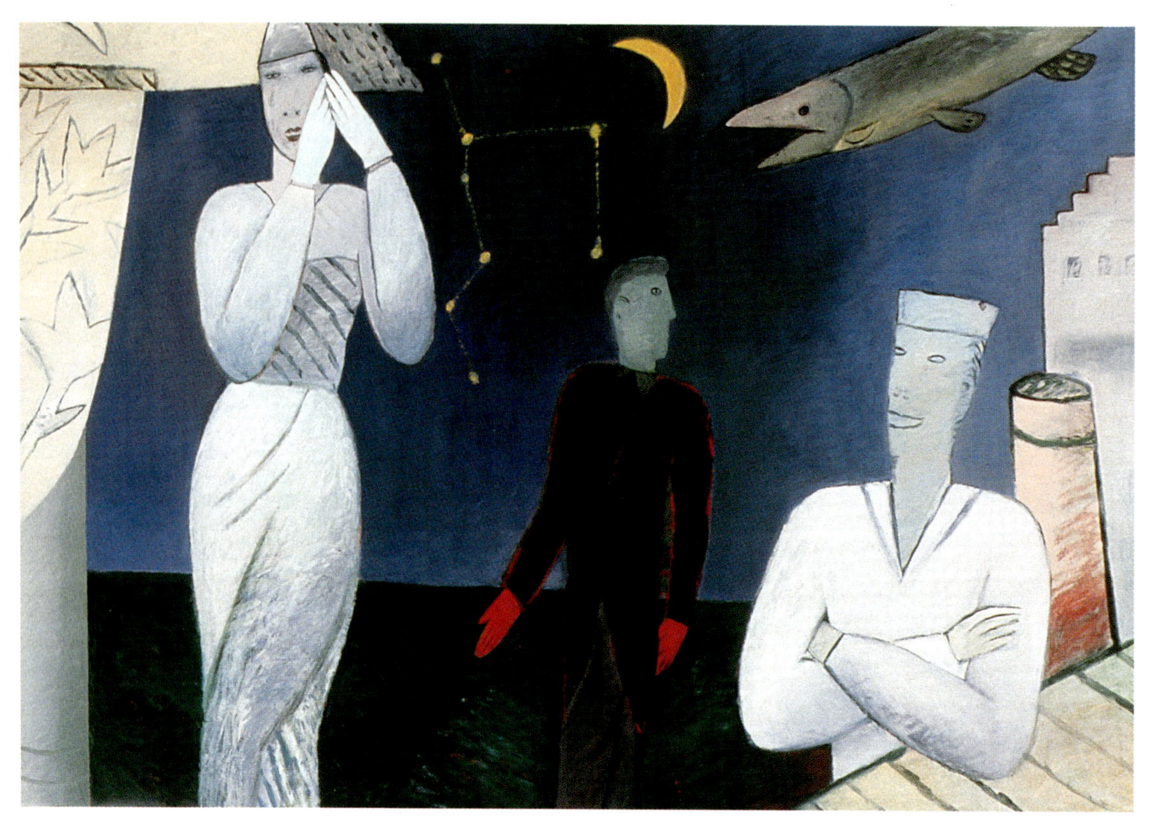

Blind Date, 1985
acrylic on paper
70" x 104"
Collection of Jill and Jay Bernstein, New York
Courtesy of Shoshana Wayne Gallery
Santa Monica, California

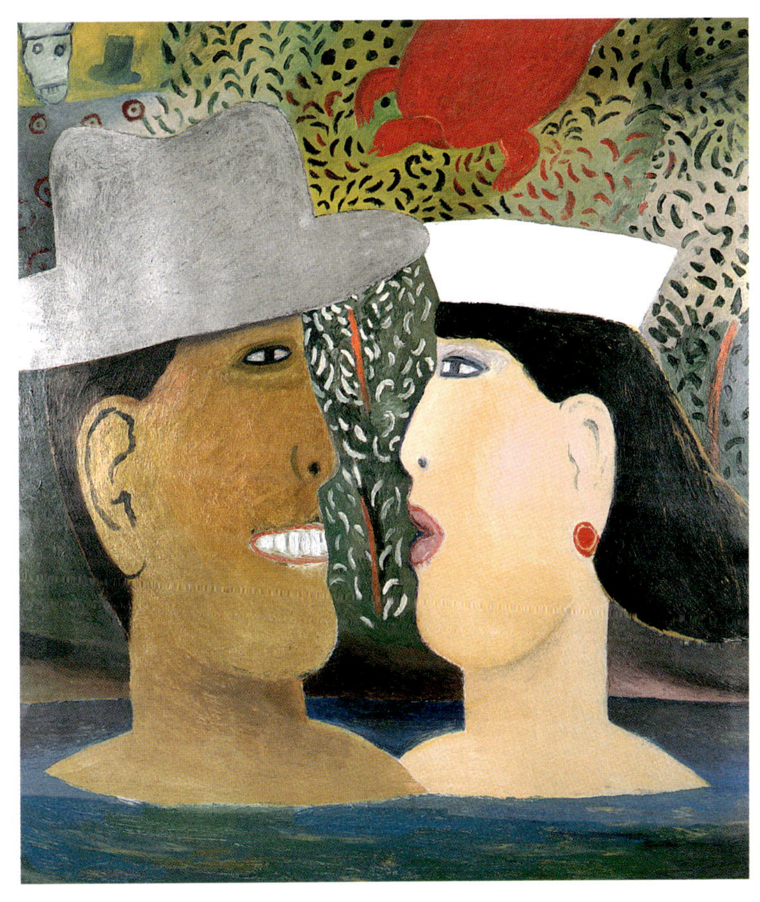

In Golden Pond, 1986
acrylic on paper
60" x 53"
Collection of Stoel Rives LLP, Attorneys
Seattle, Washington

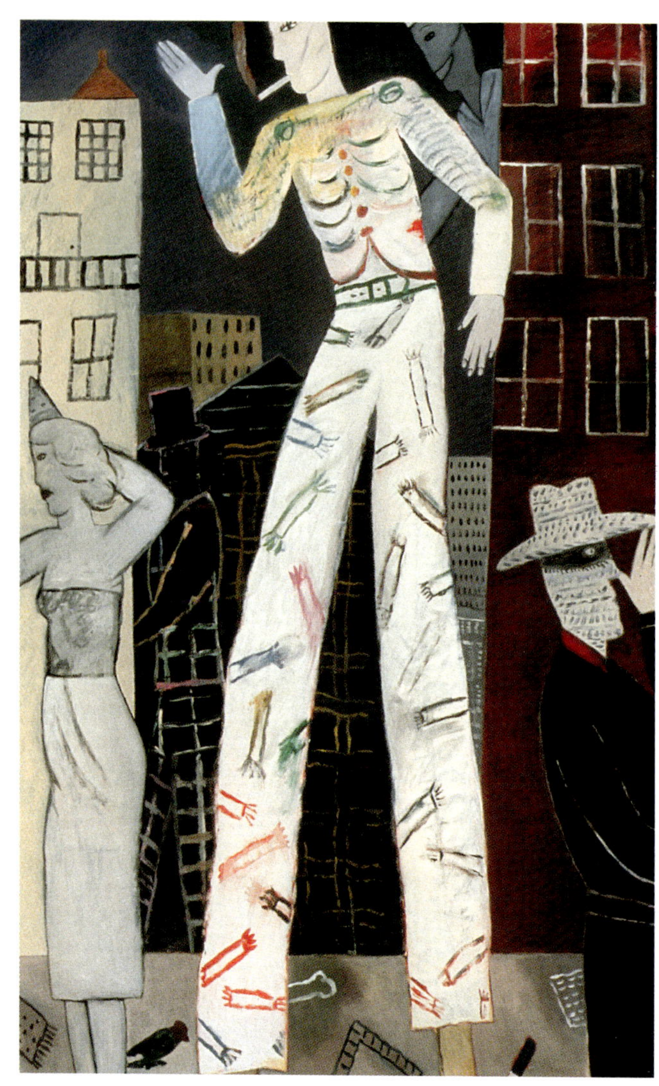

Stilt Man, 1986
acrylic on paper
96" x 60"
Courtesy of Grover/Thurston Gallery
Seattle, Washington

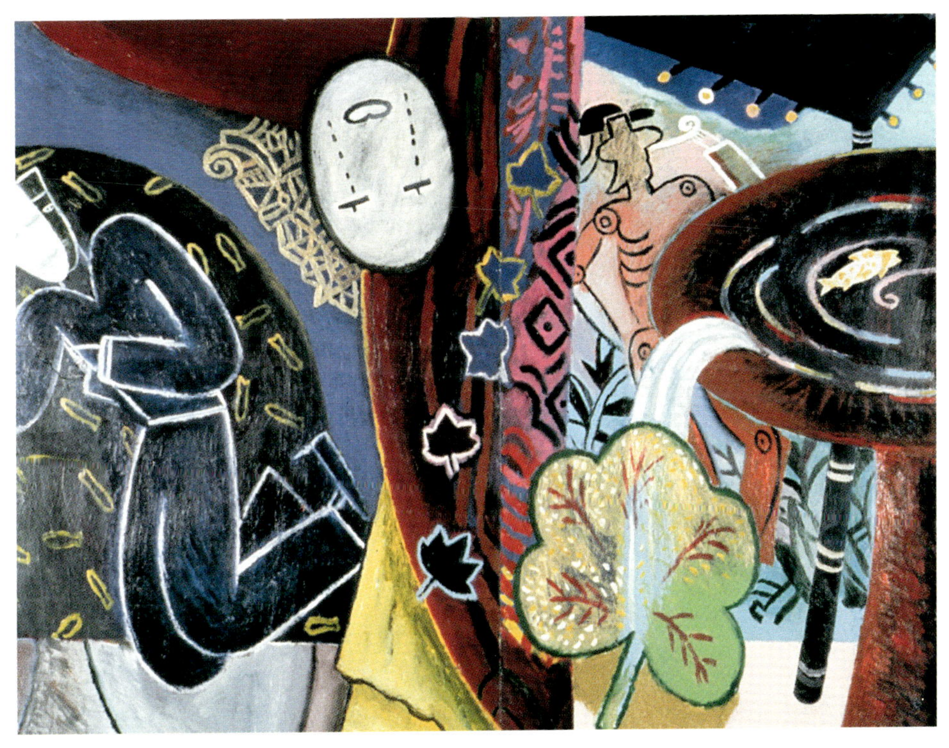

Light Sleep, 1987
acrylic on paper
39" x 50"
Collection of Daniel F. Robinson

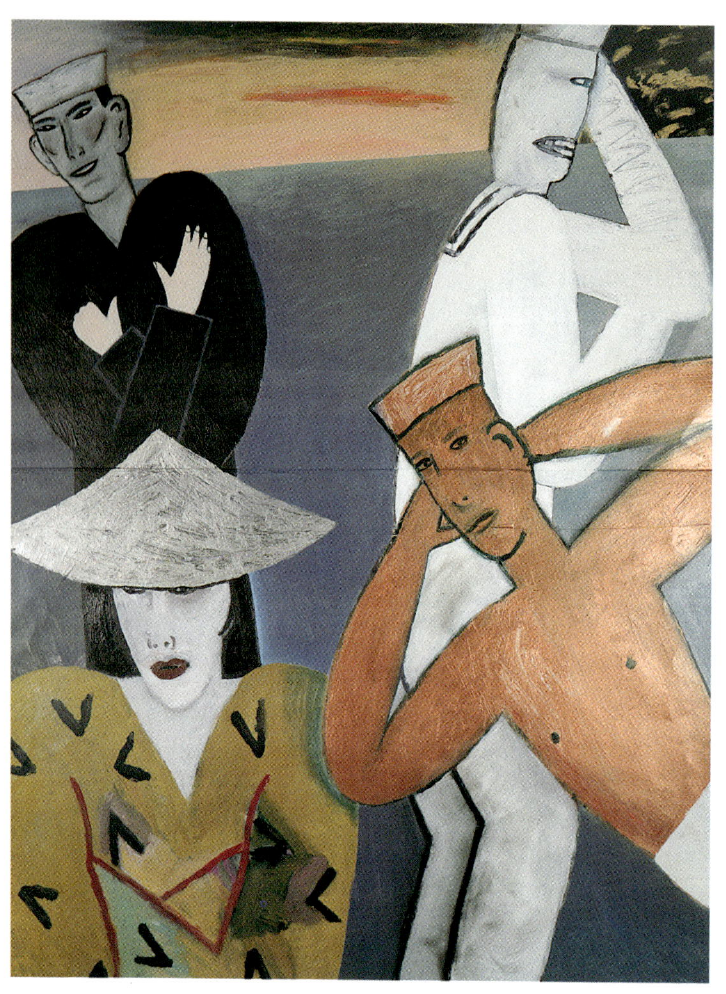

Quartet, 1987
acrylic on paper
51-1/2" x 37"
Collection of Cheney Cowles Museum
Spokane, Washington

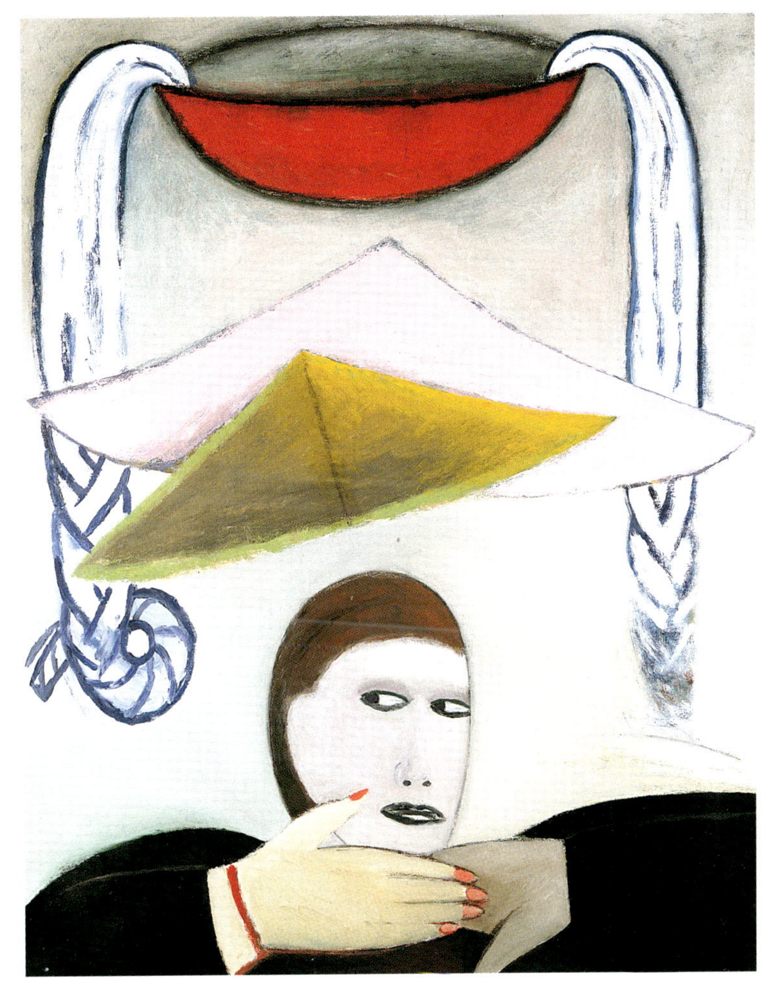

Shelter, 1987
acrylic on paper
53-1/2" x 42-1/2"
Collection of Donna Benaroya

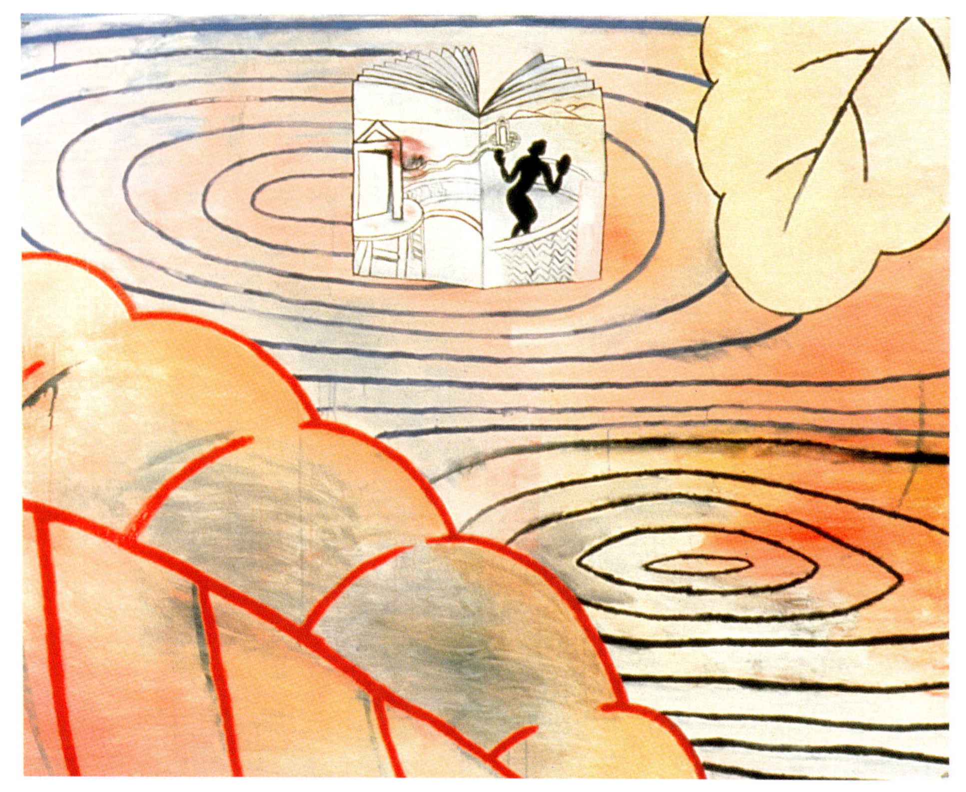

Index, 1989
acrylic and collage on paper
53" x 66"
Collection of the artist
Courtesy of Grover/Thurston Gallery
Seattle, Washington

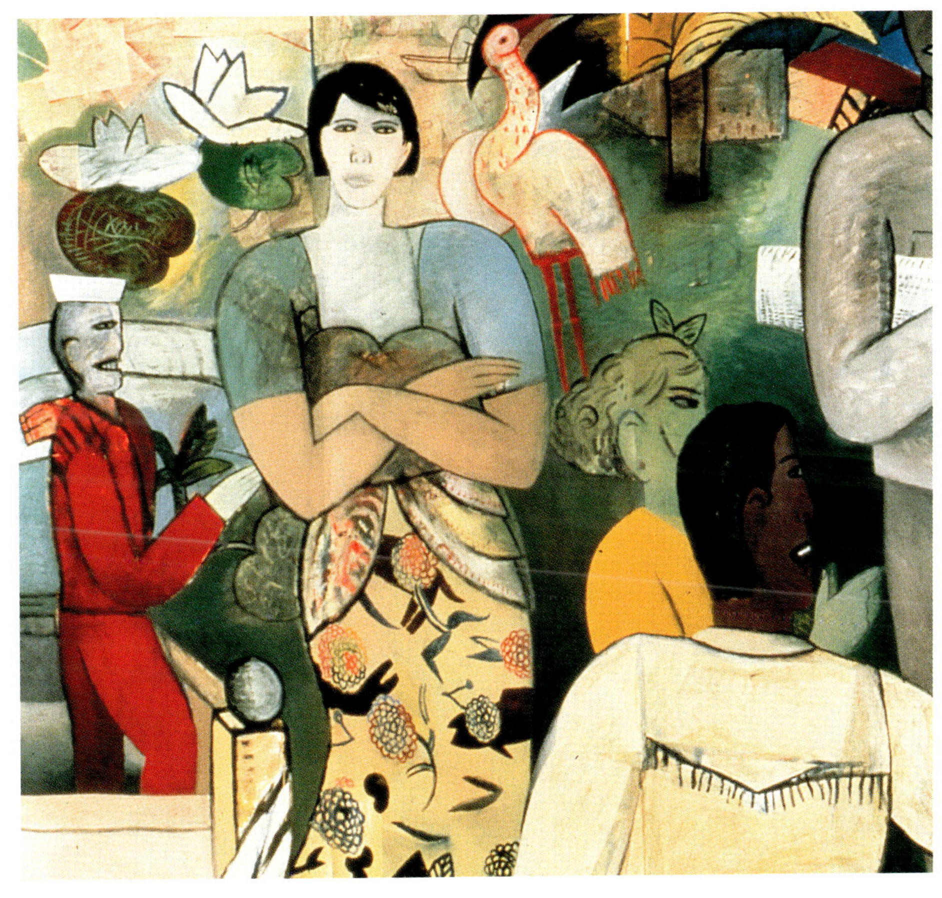

Demi-Mondaine, 1989
acrylic and collage on paper
83" x 87"
Collection of Seattle City Light 1% for Art Portable Works Collection and the Seattle Center Opera House

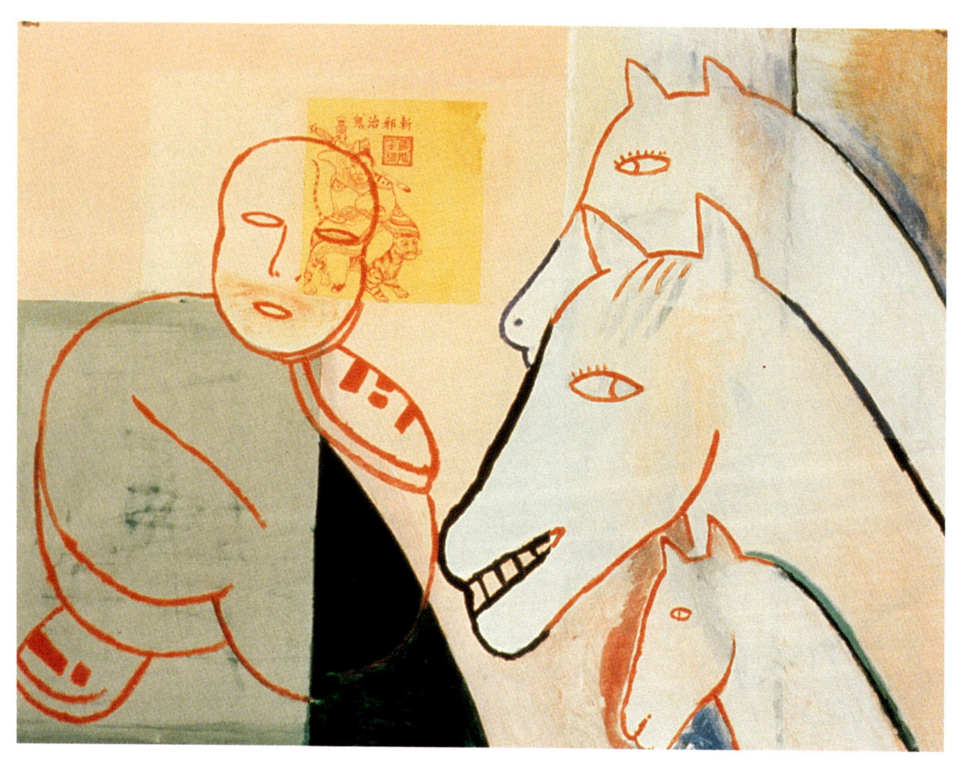

Language Lesson
(Deux Chinois et Trois Chevaux), 1989
acrylic and collage on paper
39" x 53"
Collection of Ann Gardner and Mitchell Karton

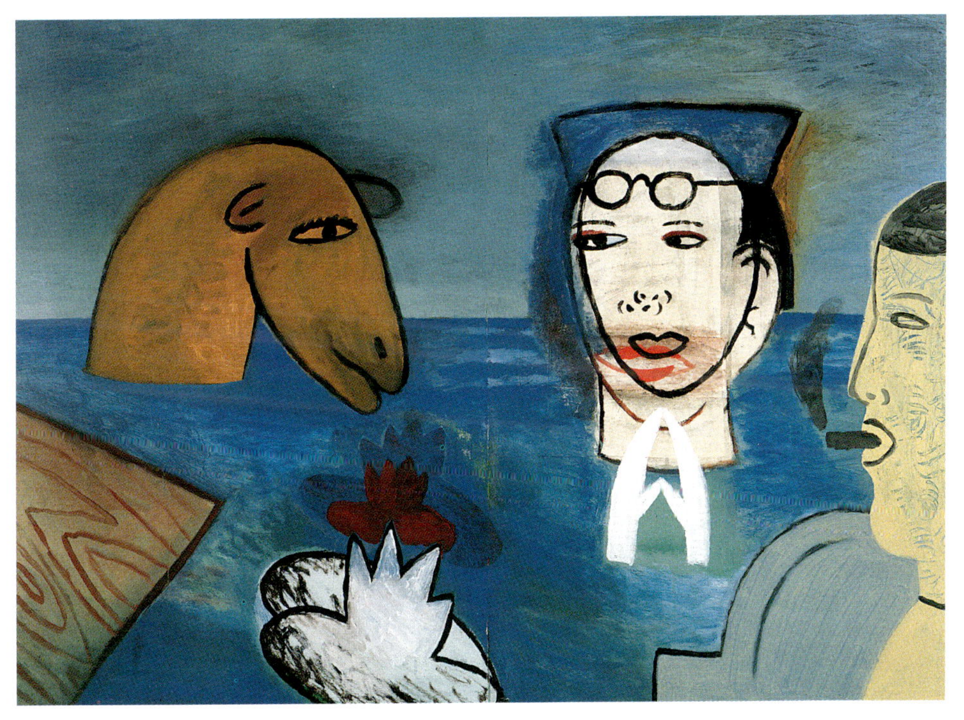

Language Lesson I, 1989
acrylic and collage on paper
39" x 50"
Collection of Gary and Mary Molyneaux

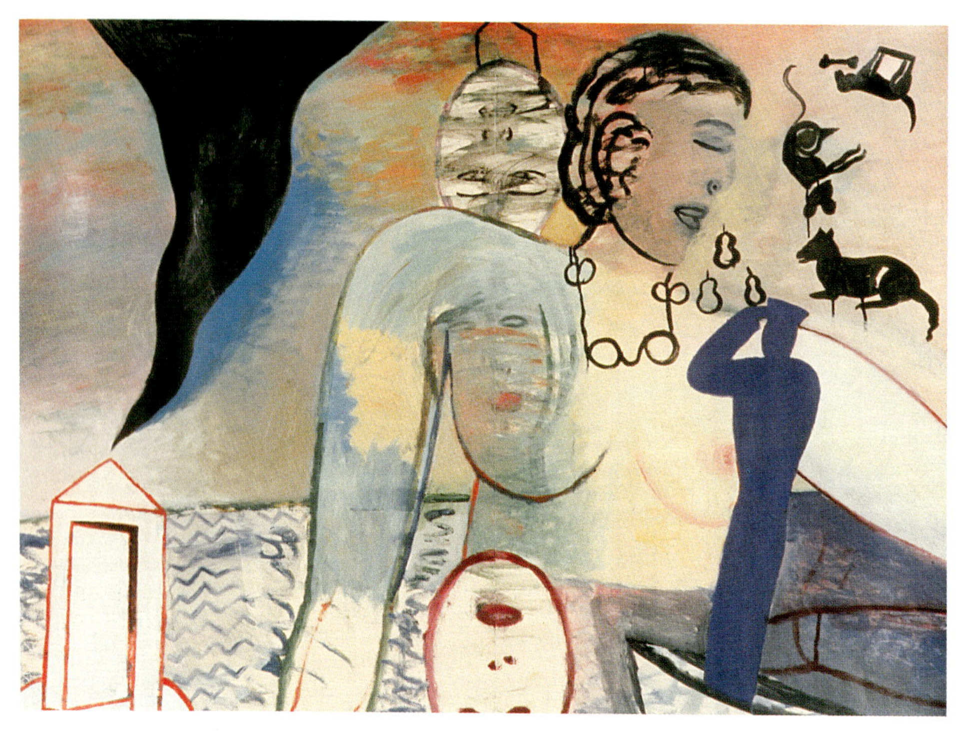

Mistral, 1989
acrylic, sumi and collage on paper
39" x 53-1/2"
Collection of J & J Wagonfeld

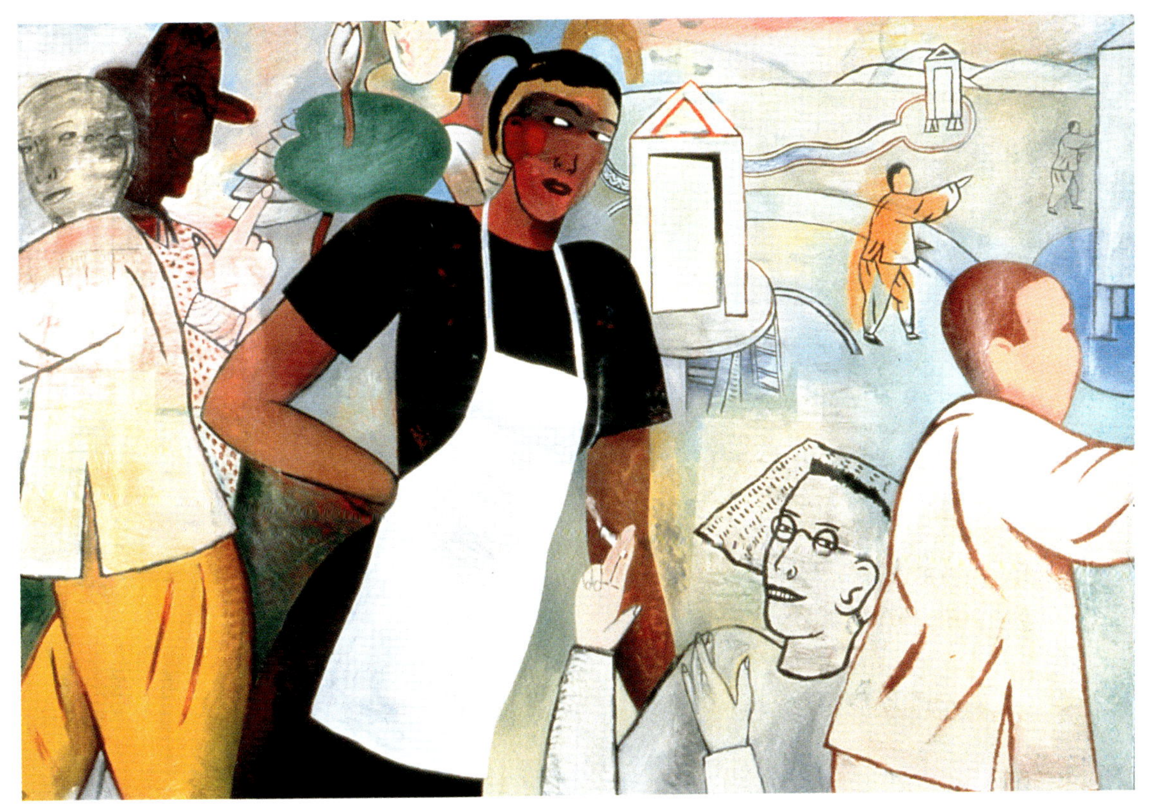

The Art Student, 1990
acrylic and collage on paper
71" x 103"
Collection of Microsoft Corporation
Redmond, Washington

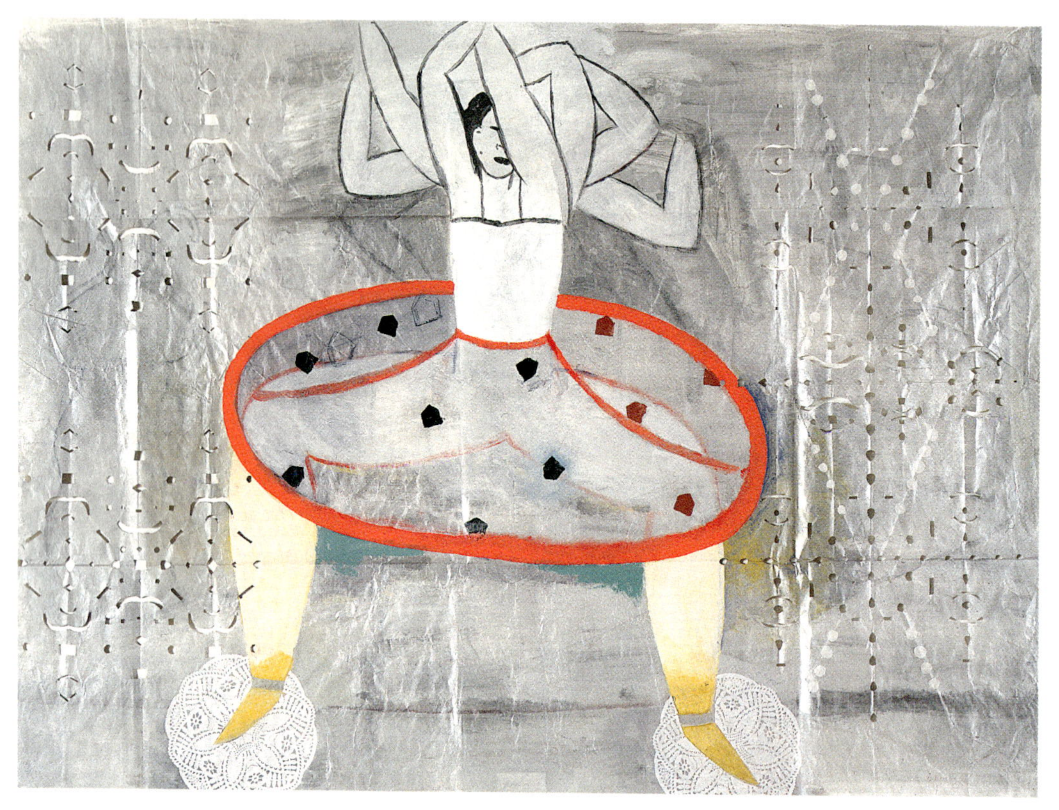

Balance, 1990
acrylic and collage on perforated paper
48" x 66"
Collection of Laurie and Scott Oki

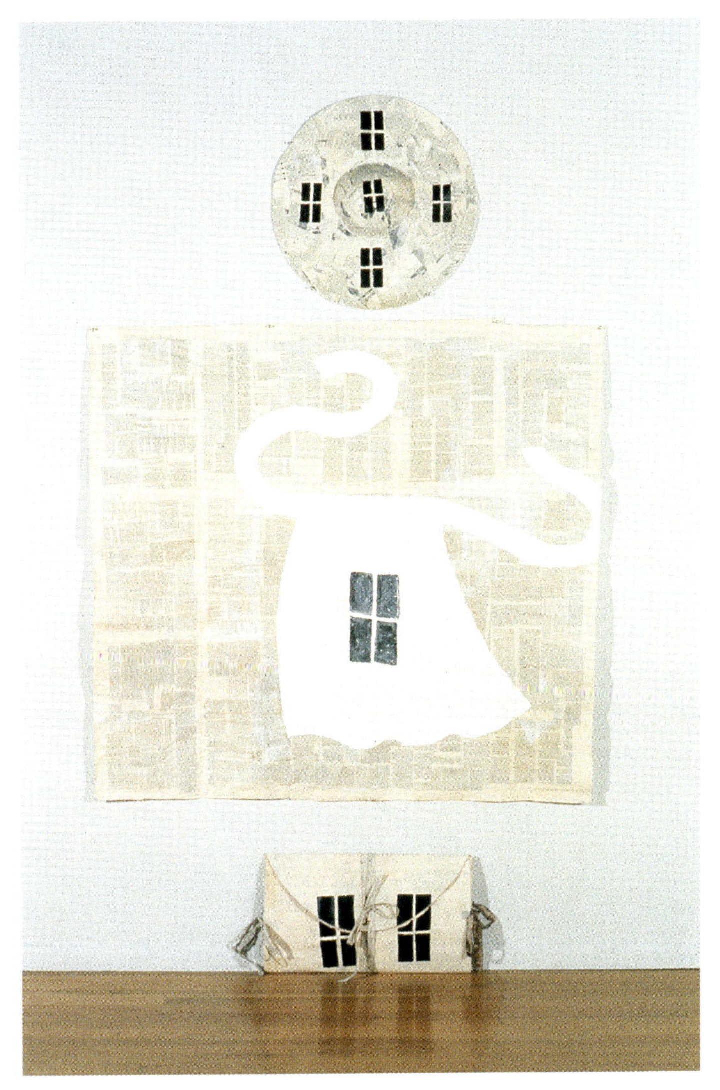

Hat, Apron, Purse**,** 1990
acrylic, cardboard, cloth tape and collage on paper
84" x 46" (3 pieces)
Collection of the artist

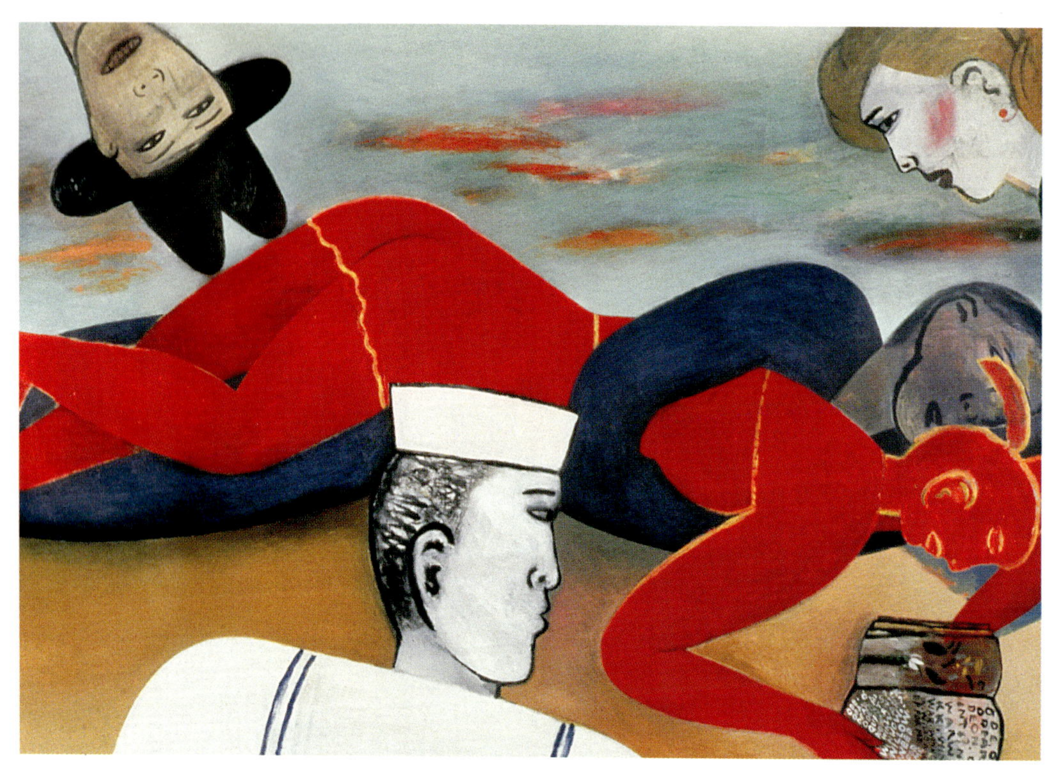

Sheet Music, 1990
acrylic and collage on paper
53" x 77"
Collection of Arlene and Harold Schnitzer

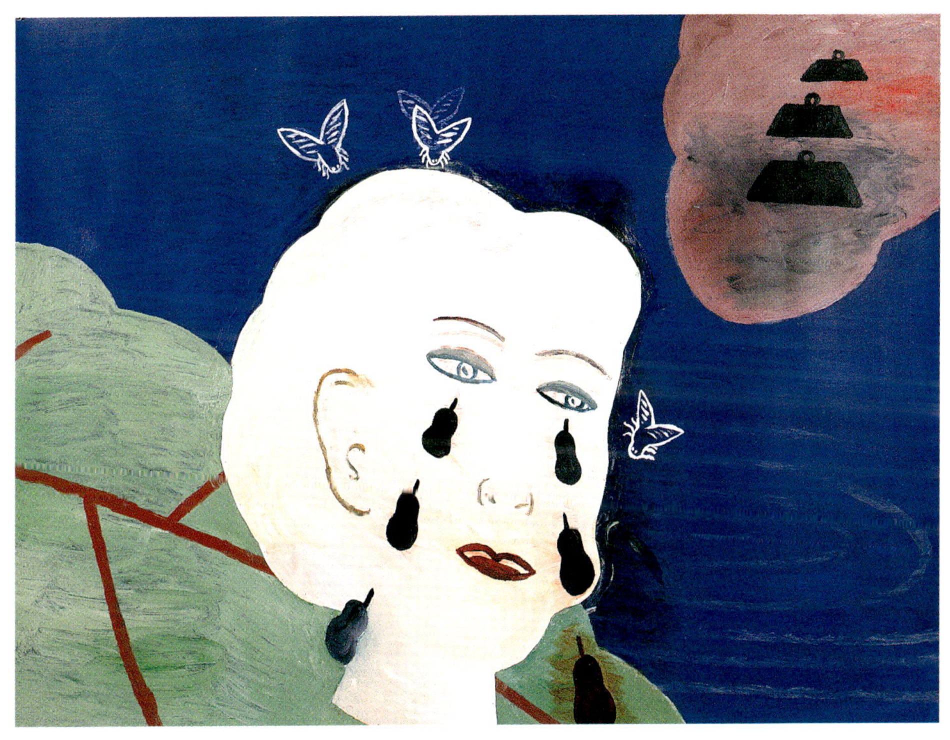

Woman Weeping Pears, 1990
acrylic and collage on paper
39-1/2" x 53"
Courtesy of the artist and the Laura Russo Gallery
Portland, Oregon

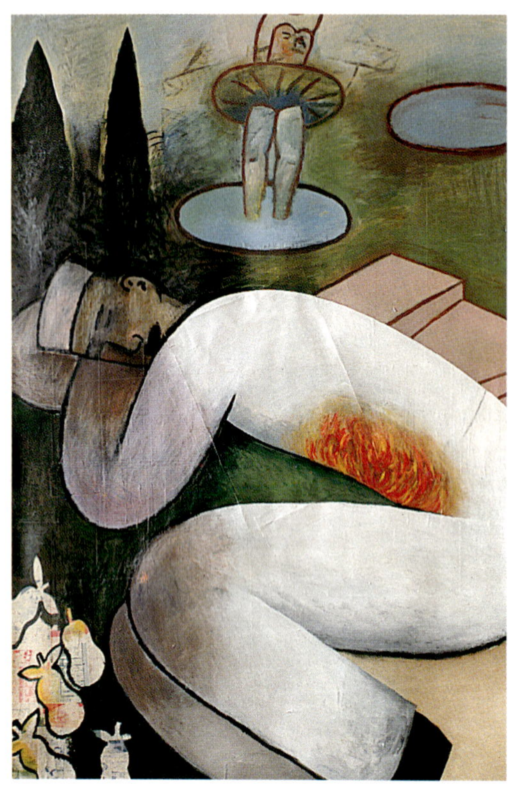
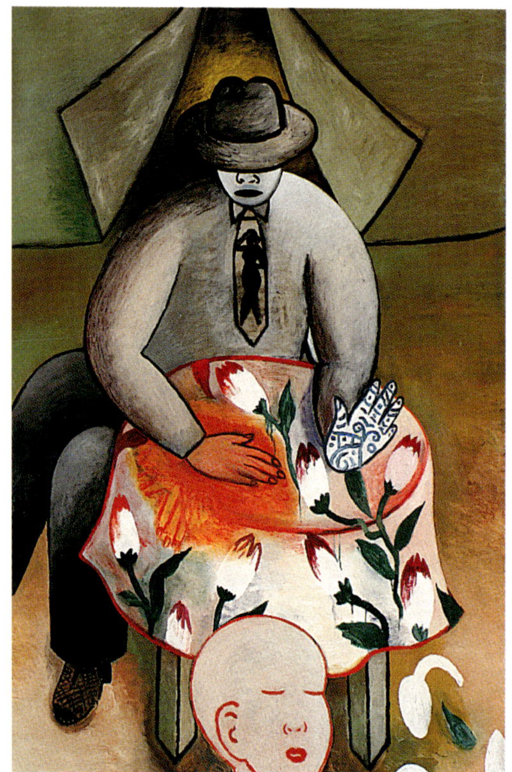
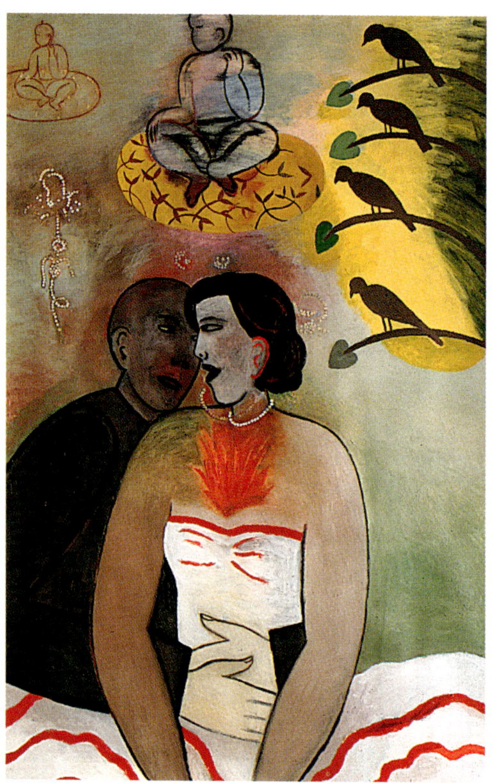

Body Fires, 1991
acrylic and collage on paper
triptych, 79" x 171"
Collection of Tacoma Art Museum, Washington
Purchased with Acquisition Funds, 92.9 a-c

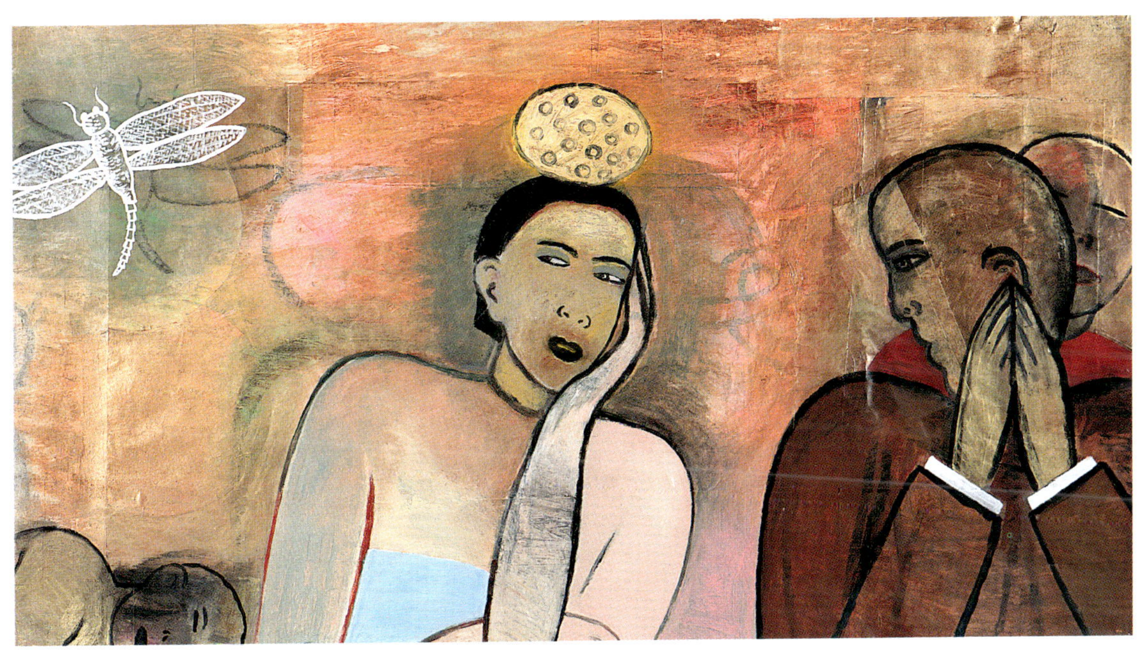

Cinema Ghost, 1991
acrylic, sumi and collage on paper
33" x 60"
Collection of Paul Schneider and Lauren Eulau

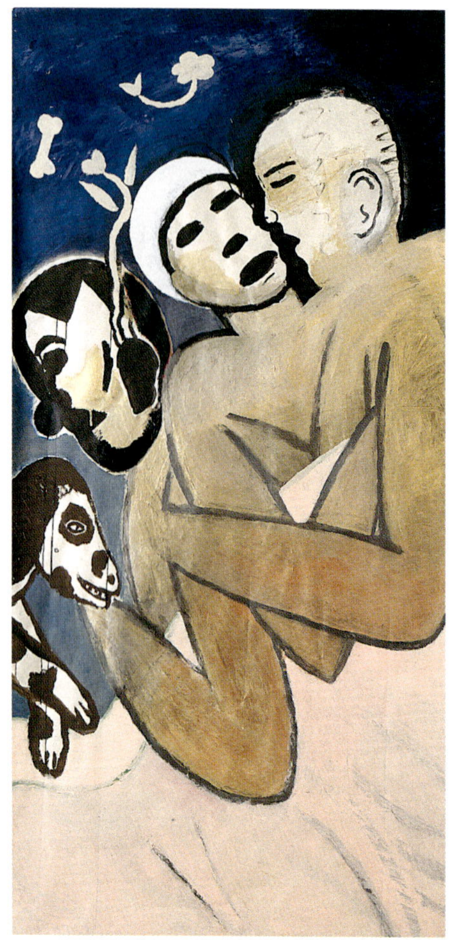

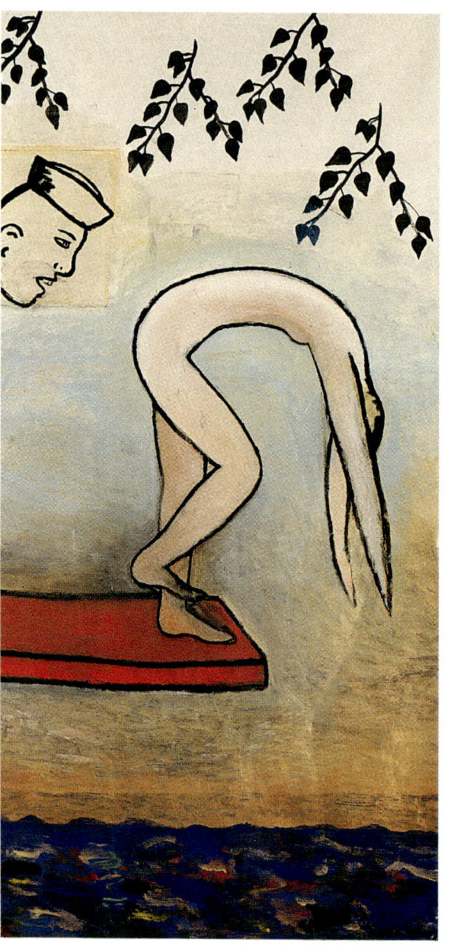

Double Jump, 1991
acrylic, sumi and collage on paper
71" x 72"
Collection of Deborah and Kenneth Novack

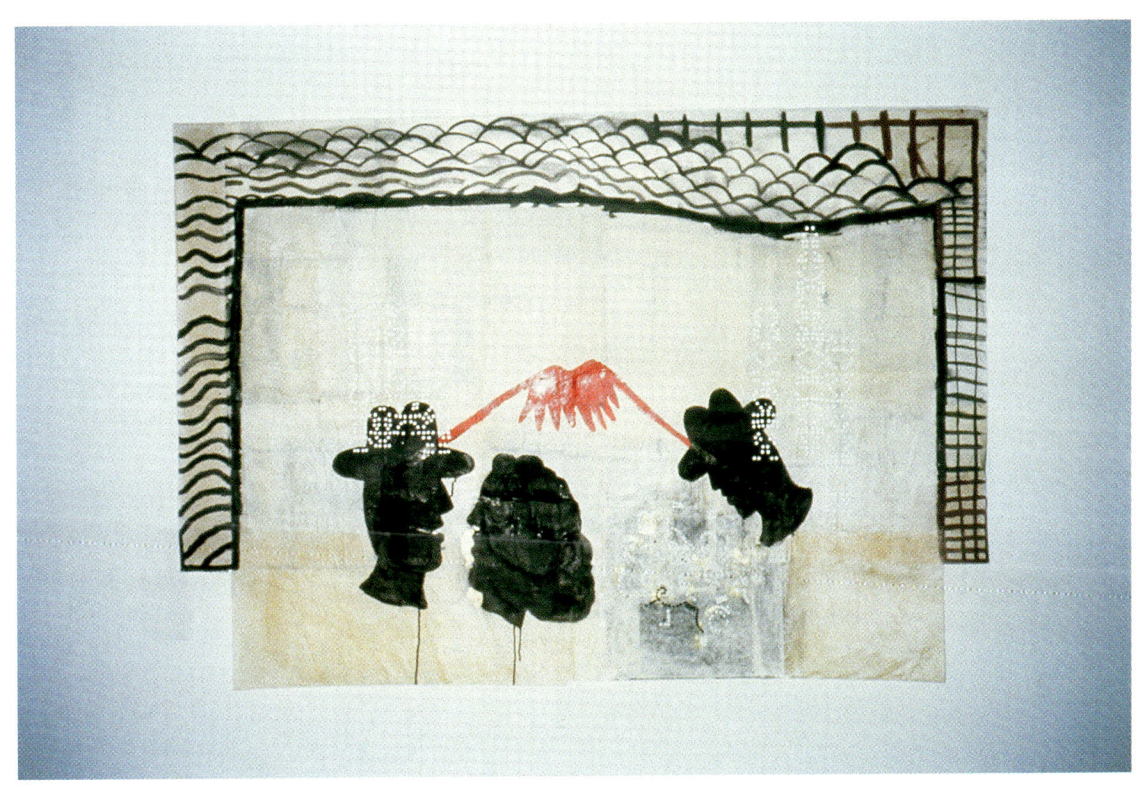

Loss, 1991
acrylic, sumi and collage on perforated paper
48" x 72"
Courtesy of Grover/Thurston Gallery
Seattle, Washington

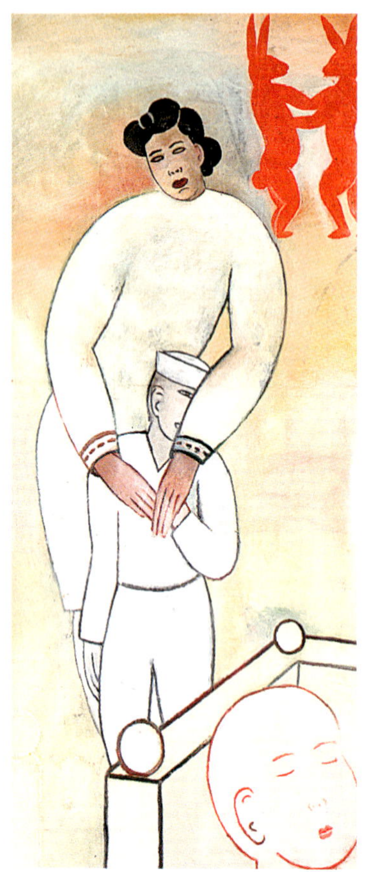

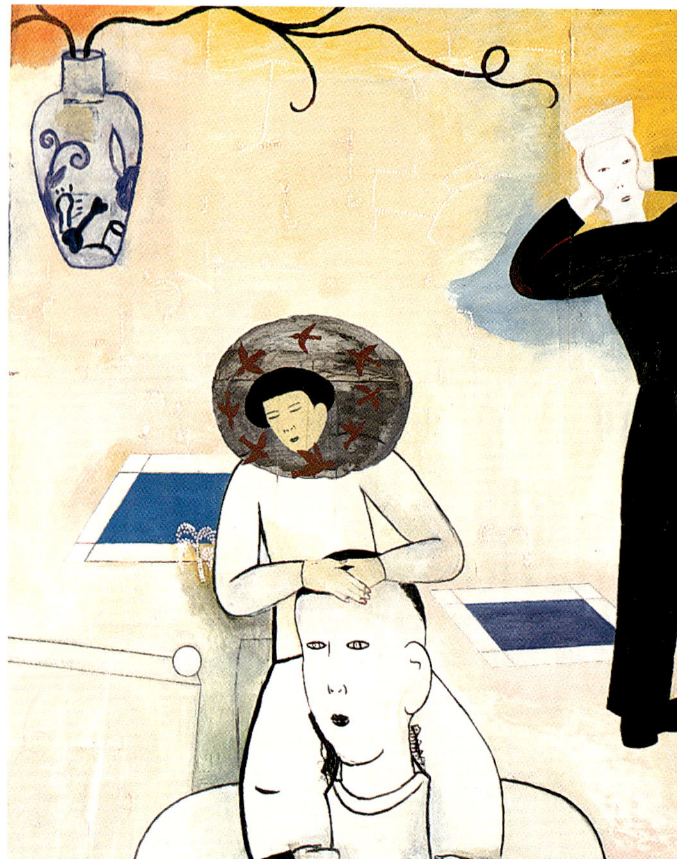

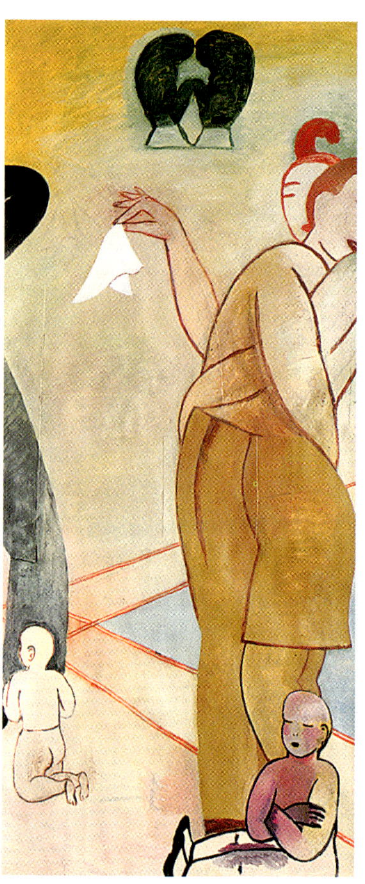

Touch & Go, 1991
acrylic, sumi and collage on paper
triptych, 88" x 157"
Collection of Nishino, Seattle, Washington

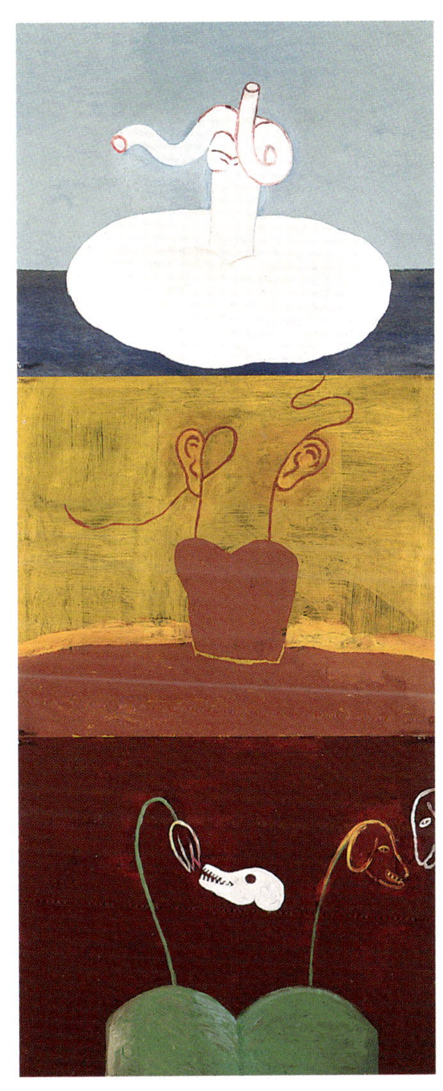

Carapace(s), 1992
acrylic on paper
72" x 30"
Collection of Dianne Elliott

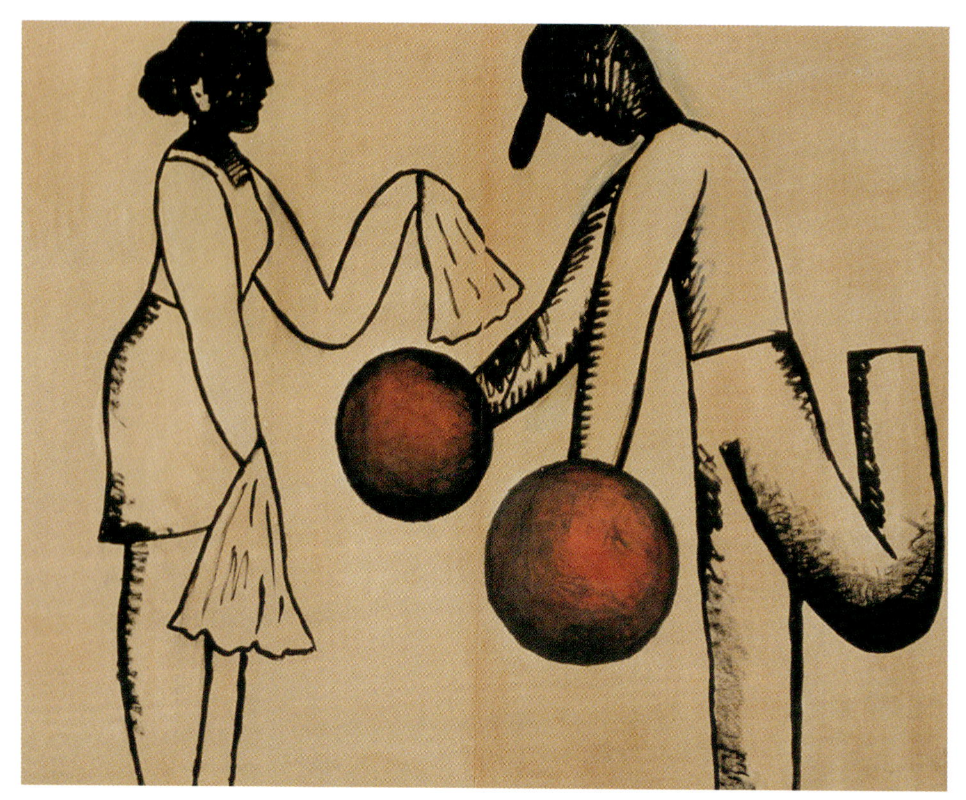

Gifts, 1992
sumi and acrylic on paper
39" x 48-1/2"
Collection of Ronald and Carol Margolis, Ltd. Partnership

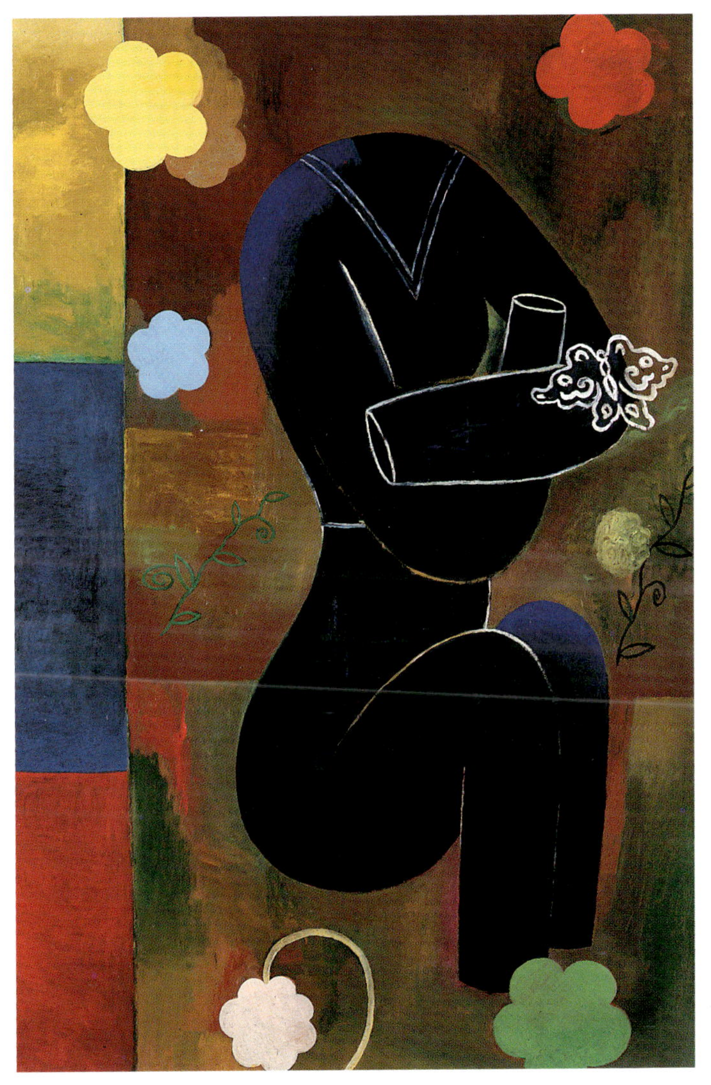

Self Portrait: Dog Bone Sailor Suit, 1992
acrylic on paper
77" x 53-1/2"
Collection of Douglas and Lila Goodman

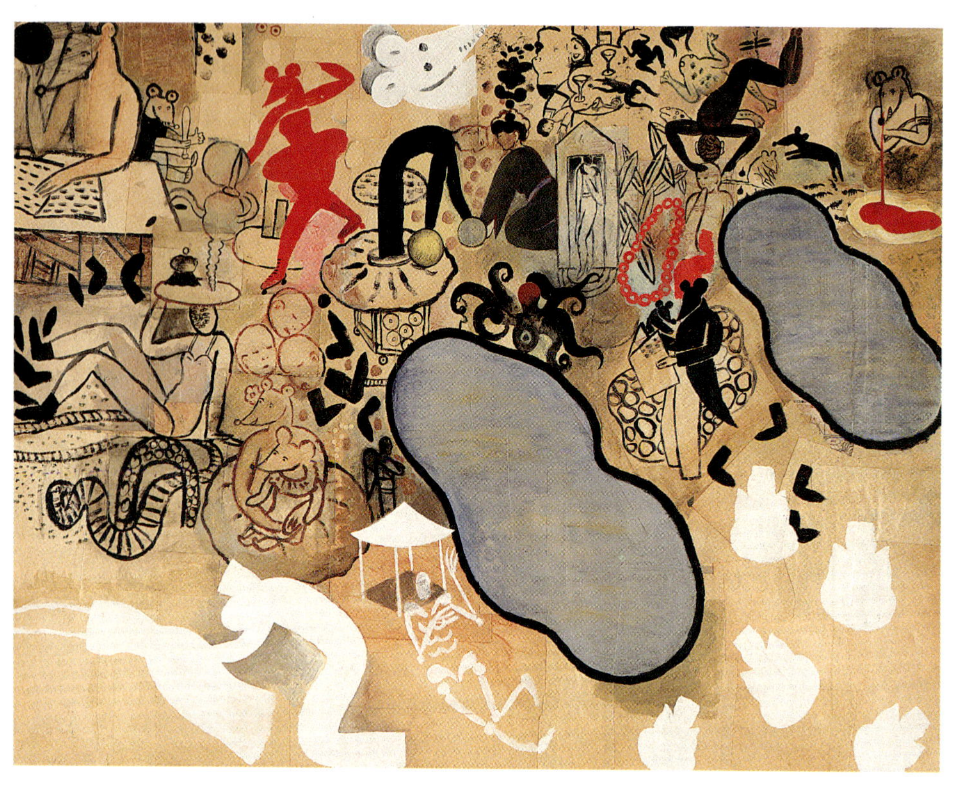

Two Pools: Riddle and Ghosts, 1992
sumi, acrylic and collage on paper
39" x 50"
Collection of the artist

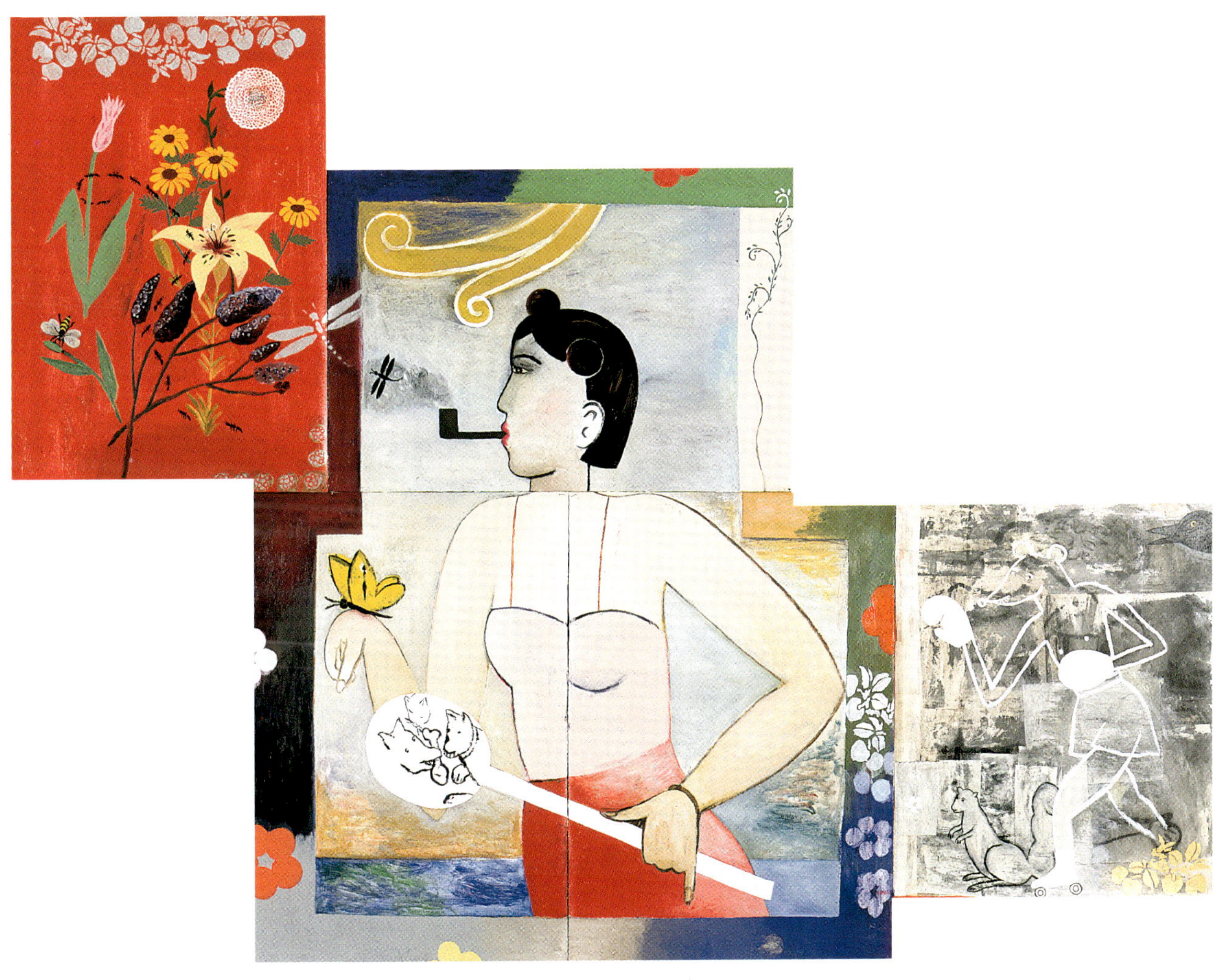

Unpeaceful Coexistence, 1993
acrylic and collage on paper
78" x 103"
Collection of Jo Bar & Rotisserie, Portland, Oregon

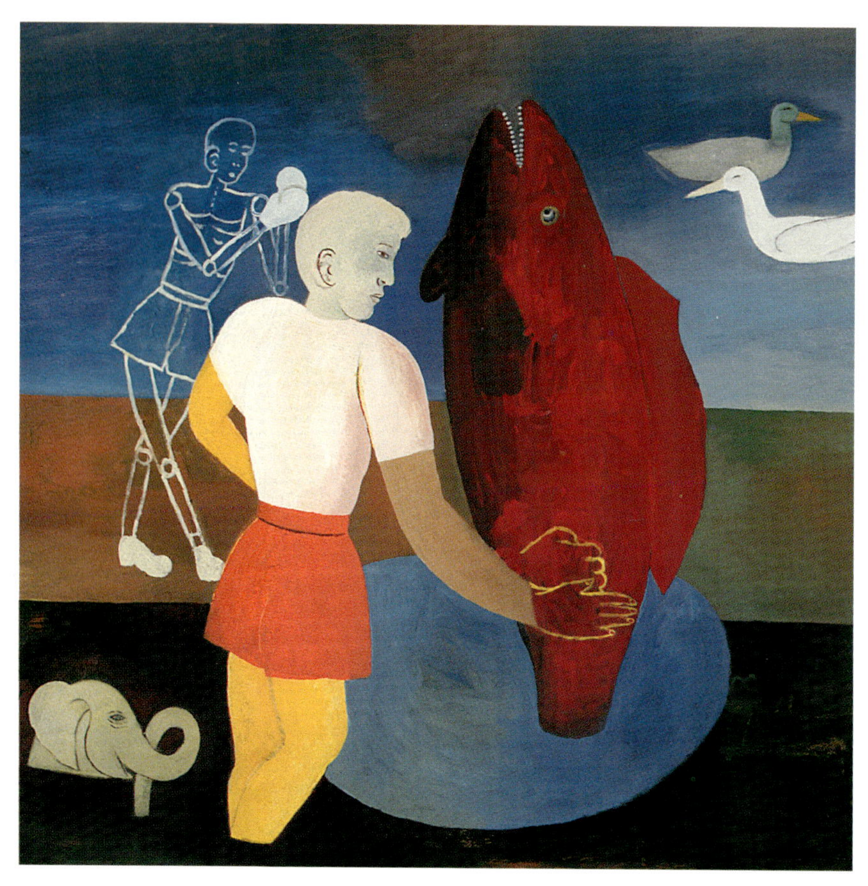

Big Fish, Small Pond, 1995
acrylic on paper
53" x 53"
Courtesy of Grover/Thurston Gallery
Seattle, Washington

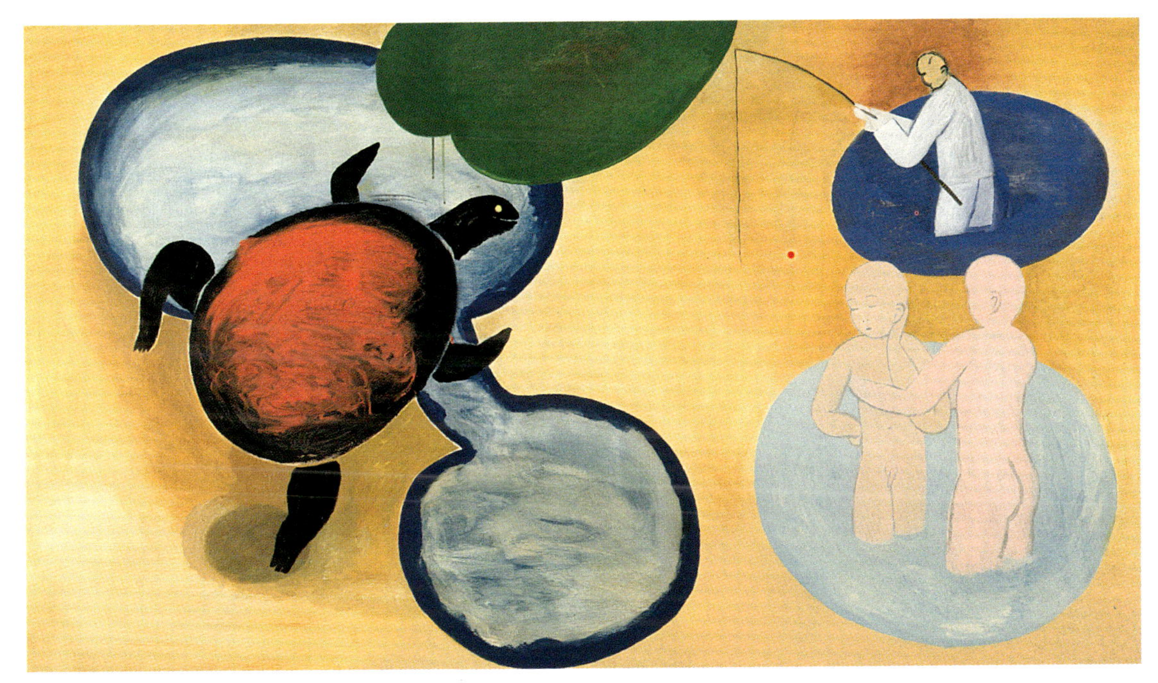

Occupied Pools, 1995
acrylic on paper
44" x 78"
Private Collection

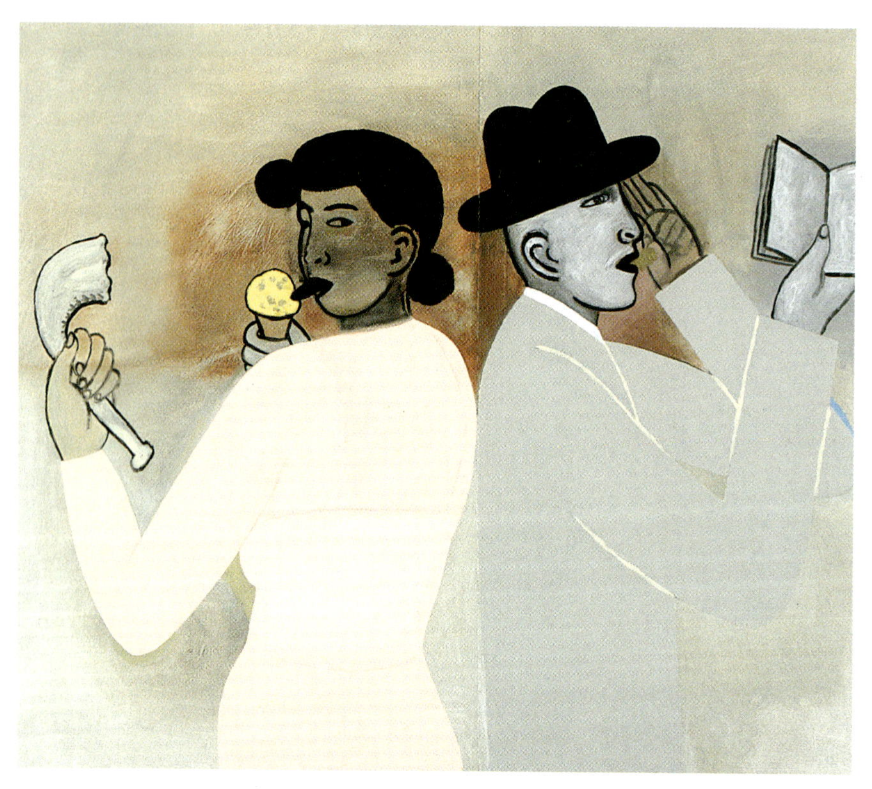

Souvenir, 1996
sumi and acrylic on Egyptian cotton on paper
mounted on wood
51-3/4" x 60"
Collection of J & J Wagonfeld

Exhibition Checklist

Salmon Man, 1973
acrylic on wood
11" x 7"
Collection of Jon Gierlich

Crows, Scarecrows, 1974
acrylic and graphite on paper
10" x 9-1/8"
Collection of Francine Seders

Picnic Spanning Three Seasons, 1974
acrylic on paper
20" x 17"
Collection of Sondra and Robert Shulman

Dance on Thin Ice, 1975
acrylic on paper
10" x 11"
Collection of Dave Hornor and Patti Jones

Nov. 22, 1976, 1978
acrylic on paper
15" x 20"
Collection of Juliana and Paul Heyne

Past & Future Dos a Dos, 1980
acrylic on paper
53" x 47"
Collection of the artist

Pink House, Off Season, 1980
acrylic on paper
52-3/4" x 47-1/4"
Collection of Timothy F. and Susan M. Jones

Bird Cage, 1981
acrylic on paper
triptych, 52-1/2" x 137-3/8"
Private Collection

Rocco & the Stone Boat, 1983
acrylic on paper
27-1/2"x 39"
Collection of Hattie and Davis Freeman

Siesta, Villa Carlotta, 1983
acrylic on paper
27-1/2" x 39"
Collection of Isabel Sim Hamilton and Charles S. Hamilton

Tragic and Comedic Queens, 1984
acrylic on paper
66" x 52-1/2"
Collection of Joel Schumacher

Alice Meets Betty, 1985
acrylic and collage on paper
27" x 39"
Collection of Markovitz/Millett

Alice vs. Betty, 1985
acrylic and collage on paper
39" x 53"
Collection of Sonja Blomdahl and Dick Weiss

Blind Date, 1985
acrylic on paper
70" x 104"
Collection of Jill and Jay Bernstein, New York
Courtesy of Shoshana Wayne Gallery, Santa Monica, California

In Golden Pond, 1986
acrylic on paper
60" x 53"
Collection of Stoel Rives LLP, Attorneys, Seattle, Washington

Stilt Man, 1986
acrylic on paper
96" x 60"
Courtesy of Grover/Thurston Gallery, Seattle, Washington

Light Sleep, 1987
acrylic on paper
39" x 50"
Collection of Daniel F. Robinson

Quartet, 1987
acrylic on paper
51-1/2" x 37"
Collection of Cheney Cowles Museum, Spokane, Washington

Shelter, 1987
acrylic on paper
53-1/2" x 42-1/2"
Collection of Donna Benaroya

Index, 1989
acrylic and collage on paper
53" x 66"
Collection of the artist
Courtesy of Grover/Thurston Gallery Seattle, Washington

Demi-Mondaine, 1989
acrylic and collage on paper
83" x 87"
Collection of Seattle City Light 1% for Art Portable Works Collection and the Seattle Center Opera House

Language Lesson (Deux Chinois et Trois Chevaux) 1989
acrylic and collage on paper
39" x 53"
Collection of Ann Gardner and Mitchell Karton

Language Lesson I, 1989
acrylic and collage on paper
39" x 50"
Collection of Gary and Mary Molyneaux

Mistral, 1989
acrylic, sumi and collage on paper
39" x 53-1/2"
Collection of J & J Wagonfeld

The Art Student, 1990
acrylic and collage on paper
71" x 103"
Collection of Microsoft Corporation Redmond, Washington

Balance, 1990
acrylic and collage on perforated paper
48" x 66"
Collection of Laurie and Scott Oki

Hat, Apron, Purse, 1990
acrylic, cardboard, cloth tape and collage on paper
84" x 46" (3 pieces)
Collection of the artist

Sheet Music, 1990
acrylic and collage on paper
53" x 77"
Collection of Arlene and Harold Schnitzer

Woman Weeping Pears, 1990
acrylic and collage on paper
39-1/2" x 53"
Courtesy of the artist and the Laura Russo Gallery, Portland, Oregon

Body Fires, 1991
acrylic and collage on paper
triptych, 79" x 171"
Collection of Tacoma Art Museum, Tacoma, Washington
Purchased with Acquisition Funds 92.9 a-c

Cinema Ghost, 1991
acrylic, sumi and collage on paper
33" x 60"
Collection of Paul Schneider and Lauren Eulau

Double Jump, 1991
acrylic, sumi and collage on paper
71" x 72"
Collection of Deborah and Kenneth Novack

Loss, 1991
acrylic, sumi and collage on perforated paper
48" x 72"
Courtesy of Grover/Thurston Gallery, Seattle, Washington

Touch & Go, 1991
acrylic, sumi and collage on paper
triptych, 88" x 157"
Collection of Nishino Seattle, Washington

Carapace(s), 1992
acrylic on paper
72" x 30"
Collection of Dianne Elliott

Gifts, 1992
sumi and acrylic on paper
39" x 48-1/2"
Collection of Ronald and Carol Margolis, Ltd. Partnership

Self Portrait: Braque Boxing, 1992
acrylic on paper
77" x 53-1/2"
Collection of Boise Art Museum Collectors Forum Purchase

Self Portrait: Dog Bone Sailor Suit, 1992
acrylic on paper
77" x 53-1/2"
Collection of Douglas and Lila Goodman

Two Pools: Riddle and Ghosts, 1992
sumi, acrylic and collage on paper
39" x 50"
Collection of the artist

Unpeaceful Coexistence, 1993
acrylic and collage on paper
78" x 103"
Collection of Jo Bar & Rotisserie Portland, Oregon

Big Fish, Small Pond, 1995
acrylic on paper
53" x 53"
Courtesy of Grover/Thurston Gallery, Seattle, Washington

Occupied Pools, 1995
acrylic on paper
44" x 78"
Private Collection

Souvenir, 1996
sumi and acrylic on Egyptian cotton on paper mounted on wood
51-3/4" x 60"
Collection of J & J Wagonfeld

Fay Jones

BORN 1936, Boston, MA
RESIDES Seattle, WA

EDUCATION

1957 B.F.A., Rhode Island School of Design, Providence, RI

SOLO EXHIBITIONS

1996 Grover/Thurston Gallery, Seattle, WA
Boise Art Museum, Boise, ID
(1997, Washington State University, Seattle Art Museum)
1994 Laura Russo Gallery, Portland, OR (also 1992, 1988)
1993 Francine Seders Gallery, Seattle, WA
(also 1990, 1989, 1987, 1985, 1982/83, 1981,
1980, 1978, 1976, 1973, 1970)
1992 Sarah Spurgeon Gallery, Central Washington University,
Ellensburg, WA
1991 Shoshana Wayne Gallery, Los Angeles, CA
(also 1989, 1986)
1990 Whatcom Museum, Bellingham, WA
1987 Spokane Falls Community College, Visual Arts Gallery,
Spokane, WA
1985 Seattle Art Museum, Seattle, WA, Documents Northwest
Series: Fay Jones
Portland Center for the Visual Arts, Portland, OR
1984 Wentz Gallery, Pacific Northwest College of Art,
Portland, OR
1983 Brunswick Gallery, Missoula, MT
1979 Viking Union Gallery, Western Washington University,
Bellingham, WA
1974 Tacoma Art Museum, Tacoma, WA

SELECTED GROUP EXHIBITIONS

1995 *Ex Libris*, Fisher Gallery, Cornish College of the Arts,
Seattle, WA
The Curatorial Eye of James Archer, Archer Gallery,
Clark College, Vancouver, WA
Carved & Incised: Contemporary Block Prints,
Whatcom Museum, Bellingham, WA
Washington: 100 Years, 100 Paintings,
Bellevue Art Museum, Bellevue, WA
1994 *Tacoma Art Museum: Selections from the Northwest
Collection*, Seafirst Gallery, Seattle, WA
1993/94 *Time Away, Selected Prints from the Artist Residency
Program of the Centrum Foundation*,
Tacoma Art Museum, Tacoma,WA
1993 *Tribute, In Remembrance of Dr. William Sawyer,
1920-1993*, William Sawyer Gallery, San Francisco, CA
The Art of Microsoft, Henry Art Gallery,
University of Washington, Seattle, WA
Two Person Show, Confluence Gallery,
Twisp Community Gallery, Twisp, WA
Northwest Art: A Narrative/Figurative View,
Valley Museum of Northwest Art, La Conner, WA
Art Works for Aids, Seattle Center Pavilion, Seattle, WA
(also 1993, 1990)
Annual Works of Heart Exhibition,
Cheney Cowles Museum, Spokane, WA
(also 1992, 1991)
Seattle x 8: New Work, Seattle Art Museum Rental Sales
Gallery, Seattle, WA
*XX: An Exhibition on the Occasion of the Women's
Caucus for Art National Conference*, Francine Seders
Gallery II, Seattle, WA
1992 *Water Works*, US West New Vector Group, Bellevue, WA
The Comedy of Art, Bumbershoot, The Seattle Arts
Festival, Seattle, WA
Northwest Tales: Contemporary Narrative Painting,
Anchorage Museum of History and Art, Anchorage, AK;
University of Alaska Museum and Fairbanks Arts
Association Galleries, Fairbanks, AK; Alaska State
Museum, Juneau, AK
Multiples, Who We Are: Autobiographies in Art, Rotunda
of the State Capitol, Olympia, WA
It Figures, The Human Image in Art, Index Gallery,
Clark College, Vancouver, WA
1991-1994 *Collaborators*, Tacoma Art Museum, Tacoma, WA
Pleas and Thank Yous, True Stories, Galleria Potatohead,
Seattle, WA; Western Gallery, Western Washington
University, Bellingham, WA; Port Angeles Fine Arts Center,
Port Angeles, WA; Cheney Cowles Memorial Museum,
Spokane, WA; Clatsop Community College, Astoria, OR; Salem
College, Winston-Salem, NC; Boise Art Museum, Boise, ID;
Steensland Gallery, St. Olaf College, Northfield, MN; Art
Department Gallery, University of Nebraska, Omaha, NE
1991 *The Artist in the Art: Self-Portraits*, Bumbershoot
Festival, Seattle Center, Seattle, WA
1991 National Governors' Association Annual Meeting
Exhibition, Washington State Convention and Trade
Center, Seattle, WA
25th Anniversary Exhibitions: The Early Years 1966-1972,
Francine Seders Gallery, Seattle, WA
Celebrations & Ceremonies, Security Pacific Gallery, Seattle, WA

War in the Gulf: From an Artist's Perspective, William Traver Gallery, Seattle, WA
Northwest Focus: Incisive Expressions, Museum of Art, Washington State University, Pullman, WA
1990 *Bumbershoot Turns 20*, Bumbershoot, The Seattle Arts Festival, Seattle, WA
Views and Visions in the Pacific Northwest, Seattle Art Museum, Seattle, WA
Work Using Recycled Materials, Francine Seders Gallery, Seattle, WA
Northwest by Southwest: Painted Fictions, Palm Springs Desert Museum, Palm Springs, CA; Yellowstone Art Center, Billings, MT; Western Washington State University, Bellingham, WA; Sarah Campbell Blaffer Gallery, University of Houston, Houston, TX
Warm Breezes, Winter Visions, Port Angeles Fine Art Center, Port Angeles, WA
1989 *100 Years of Washington Art: New Perspectives*, Tacoma Art Museum, Tacoma, WA
Two Perspectives: Fay Jones & Elizabeth Sandvig, Cheney Cowles Museum, Spokane, WA
Printmaking at Centrum, Port Angeles Fine Art Center, Port Angeles, WA
Six Northwest Women Artists, Willamette University, Salem, OR
1988 *Celebration: Especially for Children*, Bellevue Art Museum, Bellevue, WA
Paper Works, North Seattle Community College Art Gallery, Seattle, WA
In Transit: The Concept of Transport in Art, Bumbershoot, Seattle, WA
Contemporary Survey: A Visible Presence in the Northwest, Cheney Cowles Memorial Museum, Spokane, WA
1987 *Focus: Seattle*, San Jose Museum of Art, San Jose, CA
Masks: A Contemporary Perspective, Whatcom Museum of History and Art, Bellingham, WA
Private Vision/Public Spaces, Bellevue Art Museum, Bellevue, WA
1986 *A Special Premiere Exhibition*, Laura Russo Gallery, Portland, OR
Northwest Impressions: Works on Paper, Henry Art Gallery, University of Washington, Seattle, WA
The Artists and Art Forms, Henry Art Gallery, University of Washington, Seattle, WA
10/40, Anniversary Exhibition, Bellevue Art Museum, Bellevue, WA
Figure: Narrative, Whatcom Museum of History and Art, Bellingham, WA
1985 *Seattle Painting 1925-1985*, Bumberbiennale, Seattle Center, Seattle, WA
Figuration: New Image, Invitational, Fountain Gallery, Portland, OR
1984 *Strange*, Invitational, Henry Art Gallery, University of Washington, Seattle, WA
36th Annual Academy and Institute of Arts and Letters Purchase Exhibition, New York, NY
Northwest Art from Corporate Collections, Waterfront Park, Seattle, WA
1983 *Contemporary Seattle Art of the 1980s*, Bellevue Art Museum, Bellevue, WA
Bumberbiennale, Northwest Rooms, Seattle Center, Seattle, WA
Outside New York: Seattle, The New Museum, New York, NY; Seattle Art Museum, Seattle, WA
Two Person Show, Seattle Pacific University, Seattle, WA
1982 *Three from Seattle*, William Sawyer Gallery, San Francisco, CA
Women and the Environment, Gallery of Visual Arts, University of Montana, Missoula, MT
Artworks: Seattle, Bumbershoot Festival '82, Seattle Center, Seattle, WA
Introductions '82, Fountain Gallery, Portland, OR
Ten Northwest Women Artists, University of Washington Women's Information Center, Seattle, WA
Pacific Northwest Drawing Perspectives, Eastern Washington University, Cheney, WA
Northwest Collections, Henry Art Gallery, University of Washington, Seattle, WA
1981 *A Woman's Place*, John M. Kohler Arts Center, Sheboygan, WI
Seattle x 8, Open Space Gallery, Seattle, WA
Seattle Drawings: An Invitational Exhibit, Seattle Pacific University, Seattle, WA
The Mind's Eye: Expressionism, Henry Art Gallery, University of Washington, Seattle, WA
Invitational Group Exhibition, Spokane Community College, Spokane, WA
Seattle Women Artists, The Gallery, Spokane Falls Community College, Spokane, WA
1980 *Contemporary Washington State Artists*, The Cranberry Gallery, Plymouth, MA
The Artist as Magus, The Woman's Building, Los Angeles, CA
Northwest Artists: A Review, Seattle Art Museum, Seattle, WA
Three Person Show, Olympic College, Bremerton, WA
1979 *Governor's Invitational*, State Capitol Museum, Olympia, WA (also 1970)

	Washington Open, Seattle Art Museum, Seattle, WA
	Contemporary Art from Washington, Cranberry World Visitors Center, Plymouth, MA
1978	*Northwest Collectibles*, Weyerhaeuser Headquarters, Federal Way, WA (presented by the Seattle Art Museum)
	The City Collects II, Seattle Arts Commission 1% for Art Program, Seattle, WA
1977	*Robert C. Jones/Fay Jones*, Adlai Stevenson College Library, University of California, Santa Cruz, CA
	Northwest '77, Seattle Art Museum, Seattle, WA
	Seattle Walls Project, Seattle Arts Commission, Seattle, WA
1976	*Women in the Arts*, Seattle Center, Seattle, WA
	Landscapes, Francine Seders Gallery, Seattle, WA

AWARDS, GRANTS, HONORS, AND RESIDENCIES

1993	Artist in Residence, Centrum Foundation, Port Townsend, WA (also 1987)
1992	Printmaking Residency, University of Nebraska, Omaha, NE
	Artist in Residence, Pilchuck Glass School, Stanwood, WA
1990	National Endowment for the Arts, Individual Artist Fellowship Grant
1989	Two month study grant from La Napoule Art Foundation administered through Artist Trust
1984	Individual Artist Fellowship Grant, Washington State Arts Commission
1983	National Endowment for the Arts, Visual Artist Fellowship Grant

SELECTED PUBLIC AND CORPORATE COLLECTIONS

Boise Art Museum, Boise, ID
Boise State University, Boise, ID
Cheney Cowles Memorial Museum, Spokane, WA
Davis Wright Tremaine, Seattle, WA
Foster Pepper & Shefelman, Seattle, WA
King County Arts Commission, Seattle, WA
Jo Bar & Rotisserie, Portland, OR
Leimer Cross Design, Seattle, WA
Lorig and Associates, Seattle, WA
Microsoft Corporation, Redmond, WA
Municipal Collection of the City of Seattle
Nishino, Seattle, WA
Portland Art Museum, Portland, OR
Psychoanalytic Institute, Seattle, WA
Reed, McClure, Moceri and Thonn, Seattle, WA
Seafirst Bank, Seattle, WA
Seattle Art Museum, Seattle, WA
Seattle Opera House, Seattle, WA
Stoel Rives LLP, Attorneys, Seattle, WA
Tacoma Art Museum, Tacoma, WA
University of Washington Medical Center, Seattle, WA
Vesti Corporation, Boston, MA
Washington Schools Art Collection, Washington State Arts Commission
Women's Health Care Clinic, Inc., Seattle, WA

COMMISSIONS

Bumbershoot Festival poster, Seattle, WA
Seattle Arts Commission, Seattle, WA

Selected Bibliography

CHRONOLOGICAL LIST OF BOOKS AND CATALOGUES

1996 *Fay Jones: A 20 Year Retrospective*. Boise, ID: Boise Art Museum.

1995 Allan, Lois. *Contemporary Art in the Northwest*. Roseville East, New South Wales, Australia: Craftsman House.

1993 Bruce, Chris. *The Art of Microsoft*. Seattle, WA: Henry Art Gallery, University of Washington.

1993 McLerran, Jennifer. "Narrative and Figurative Trends: Telling Differences," in Brunsman, Laura and Ruth Askey, editors, *Modernism and Beyond, Women Artists of the Pacific Northwest*. New York, NY: Midmarch Arts Press.

1990 *Art Works for AIDS*. Seattle, WA: Seattle Center Pavilion.

1990 *Northwest Originals, Washington Women and Their Art*. Portland, OR: MatriMedia

1990 *Northwest By Southwest: Painted Fictions*. Palm Springs, CA: Palm Springs Desert Museum.

1990 Johns, Barbara. *Modern Art from the Pacific Northwest in the Collection of the Seattle Art Museum*. Seattle, WA: Seattle Art Museum.

1989 Kingsbury, Martha. *Celebrating Washington's Art and Centennial Year Exhibition Guide*. Olympia, WA: 1989 Washington Centennial Commission.

1984 *Strange*. Seattle, WA: Henry Art Gallery, University of Washington.

1984 Koenig, John Franklin. *Northwest Art from Corporate Collections*. Seattle, WA: Seattle Parks Centennial Commission.

1983 Guenther, Bruce. *50 Northwest Artists*. San Francisco, CA: Chronicle Books.

1983 Lippard, Lucy. *Overlay, Contemporary Art and the Art of Prehistory*. New York, NY: Pantheon Books.

1983 Rifkin, Ned. *Outside New York: Seattle*. New York, NY and Seattle, WA: The New Museum and Seattle Art Museum.

1982 *The Washington Year: A Contemporary View, 1980-81*. Seattle, WA: Henry Art Gallery, University of Washington.

1981 *A Woman's Place*. Sheboygan, WI: John Michael Kohler Arts Center.

1977 Shulman, Sondra. *Fay Jones*. Seattle, WA: Francine Seders Gallery.

CHRONOLOGICAL LIST OF PERIODICALS

1996 Updike, Robin. "Painter of Dreams: Fay Jones Creates a Unique World." *Seattle Times*, April 21.

1996 Hackett, Regina. "It is No Stroke of Luck That Brings Fay Jones to Prominence." *Seattle Post-Intelligencer*, April 17.

1995 Hackett, Regina. "Books Take a Variety of Shapes in Artists' Hands." *Seattle Post-Intelligencer*, January 16.

1995 Frederickson, Eric and Brad Steinbacher. "Highbrow Reviews: Artists' Books and a Booker Prize Winner." *The Stranger*, January 10-16.

1993 Hackett, Regina. "A NW Tribute: The Art of Microsoft." *Seattle Post-Intelligencer*, July 1.

1993 Berger, David. "Art Friendly Microsoft may be the Region's Most Surprising Patron." *The Seattle Times/Pacific*, June 27.

1993 Kelleey, Pam. "Fay Jones at Francine Seders Gallery." *Reflex*, March/April.

1993 Hackett, Regina. "Fay Jones' Paintings Read Like Novels." *Seattle Post-Intelligencer*, February 22.

1993 Hackett, Regina. "Individualists' Styles Share the Spotlight in Show of Women Artists." *Seattle Post-Intelligencer*, January 19.

1992 Pate, Suzanne. "Art Show Tells '100 True Stories' of Personal Dreams." *The Spokesman Review-Spokane Chronicle*, March 6.

1992 Hutton, Jean. "Fay Jones at Laura Russo Gallery." *Reflex*, March/April.

1992 Ingram, Jan. "Northwest Narrative Artists are Good Story in Themselves." *Anchorage Daily News*, February 23.

1992 Gragg, Randy. "Hit Parade, Latest Works Display Fay Jones' Continuing Strength." *The Oregonian*, February 14.

1992 Gragg, Randy. *The Oregonian*, February 5.

1992 Cover art in *Reflex*, January/February.

1991 Domini, John. "Tides of Change, Art of the Pacific Northwest." *Antiques & Fine Art*, September/October.

1991 Hackett, Regina. "Seders' 25th Anniversary Show Starts off with a Sterling Exhibit." *Seattle Post-Intelligencer*, May 16.

1991 Hackett, Regina. " 'Celebrations & Ceremonies' Lifts the Veil from Wedded Bliss." *Seattle Post-Intelligencer*, May 8.

1991 Hackett, Regina. "Tacoma Art Museum Scores with Exhibit of Teamwork." *Seattle Post-Intelligencer*, April 17.

1991 Raether, Keith. "The Art of Collaboration." *Tacoma Morning News Tribune*, April 14.

1991 Mathieson, Karen. "War Within and Without." *The Seattle Times*, March 7.

1991 Carlsson, Jae. "Fay Jones, Whatcom Museum." *Artforum International*, February.

1990 Kangas, Matthew. "Stories of our Lives." *The Weekly* (Seattle, WA), October 17.

1990 Farr, Sheila. "Seattle Painter Freezes Drama into an Instant." *The Bellingham Herald*, September 30.

1990 Smallwood, Lyn. "Fetching Etchings." *The Weekly* (Seattle, WA), May 9.

1990 Smallwood, Lyn. "Fainter Paint." *The Weekly* (Seattle, WA), March 14.

1990 Hackett, Regina. "Fay Jones Has Dreamed Up a Painting Style All Her Own." *Seattle Post-Intelligencer*, March 13.

1990 Tarzan Ament, Deloris. "Jones' Collage Technique Builds Layers of Meaning." *Seattle Times*, March 9.

1990 "NEA Visual Arts Fellowships: Northwest Recipients." *Artist Trust*, March.

1990 Turner, Priscilla. "Sob Story." *Alaska Airlines Magazine*, March.

1990 Hackett, Regina. "An NEA Working Creative Magic." *Seattle Post-Intelligencer*, February 13.

1989 Bryant, Elizabeth. "The Desire to Connect." *Reflex*, November/December.

1989 Hosack, Kathy. "These Two Perspectives Are Well Worth Sharing." *Spokane*, November 12.

1989 Lane, Bob. "Tunnel Station Opens to Raves." *The Seattle Times*, August 12.

1989 Hammond, Pamela. "Fay Jones." *Artnews*, May.

1989 J.P. "Dix Jeunes Artistes en Residence de Printemps." Nice Matin, March 20.

1989 "Artist Trust Visual Artist for Residency at La Napoule in France." *Artist Trust*, Spring.

1988 "Tunnel Vision." *Seattle Times/Seattle Post-Intelligencer*, August 7.

1988 Kangas, Matthew. "Fay Jones at Francine Seders." *Art in America*, March.

1987 Schnoor, Chris. "An Eye for Inner Forces." *Reflex*, November/December.

1987 Berger, David. "Fay Jones' Palette Produces Dreamy, Complex Images." *The Seattle Times*, September 30.

1987 Smallwood, Lyn. "Fay Jones Takes an Abstract, Poetic Turn." *Seattle Post-Intelligencer*, September 15.

1986 Hackett, Regina. "Exhibit in San Jose Spotlights Seattle Art." *Seattle Post-Intelligencer*, December 19.

1986 Berkson, Bill. "Report from Seattle, In the Studios." *Art in America*, September.

1986 Connell, Joan. "Exhibit Lets Figure Tell Stories." *Bellingham Herald*, February 2.

1985 Joseph, Nancy. "Fay Jones at the Francine Seders Gallery." *Vision*, Fall.

1985 "New Acquisition." *Portland Art Association*, August.

1985 "Books in a Collage Matrix." Complimentary Anniversary Issue, *Signature*, July.

1985 Hackett, Regina. "The Words Get in the Way in These Collages." *Seattle Post-Intelligencer*, June 14.

1985 Berger, David. "Books are a Medium for Jones' Collages." *Seattle Times*, June 14.

1985 Kangas, Matthew. "Stories From the Past." *Artweek*, March 23.

1985 Smallwood, Lyn. "Figuratively Speaking." *The Weekly* (Seattle, WA), March 20-26.

1985 Berger, David. "Jones Paints Life in Vivid, Curious Vignettes." *The Seattle Times/Seattle Post-Intelligencer*, March 10.

1985 Smallwood, Lyn. "Visual Arts: Fay Jones Emerges." *The Weekly* (Seattle, WA), March 6-12.

1985 "New Paintings by Jones at Seattle Art Museum." *Art Stars*, March.

1985 Hackett, Regina. "Fine Coloration Carries the Day for Fay Jones' Paintings." *Seattle Post-Intelligencer*, February 25.

1985 Hayakawa, Alan R. "Content is Back; Much Else Absent." *The Oregonian*, February 5.

1984 Smallwood, Lyn. "Strange and Wonderful." *The Weekly* (Seattle, WA), November 28.

1984 Berger, David. "If It Seems 'Strange' Think About It." *Seattle Times*, November 16.

1984 Hackett, Regina. " 'Strange' Odd is in at UW's Henry Art Gallery." *Seattle Post-Intelligencer*, November 16.

1984 Moorman, Margaret. "Artists the Critics are Watching." *Artnews*, November.

1983 "Six Women Artists." *Seattle Woman*, December.

1983 Smallwood, Lyn. "Seattle Art from New York City." *The Weekly* (Seattle, WA), October 26.

1983 Hackett, Regina. "Paul Berger's Photos Packed with Meaning." *Seattle Post-Intelligencer*, October 20.

1983 Kendall, Sue Ann. "Home is Where the Art Is." *Seattle Times*, October 13.

1983 Hackett, Regina. "Snubbed in N.Y. Seattle Art Show Gets No Respect." *Seattle Post-Intelligencer*, October 12.

1983 Maxwell, Jessica. "Oyster Light: The Renaissance of Seattle Art." *United Airlines Magazine*, October.

1983 Smallwood, Lyn. "The Return of the Imagists." *The Weekly* (Seattle, WA), April 27.

1983 Hackett, Regina. "3 Artists: Pleasurable Still Lifes, Emotions in Color and Wild Dogs." *Seattle Post-Intelligencer*, April 22.

1982 Kendall, Sue Ann. "Love and Death Play 'the Game' in Show." *Seattle Times*, December 26.

1982 Hackett, Regina. "Seattle Artists Picked for N.Y. Show." *Seattle Post-Intelligencer*, December 22.

1981 Dike, Patricia. "Women Artists Share Visions." *The Spokesman Review*, May 17.

1980 Hackett, Regina. "Raising a Few Hackles Amid Show's Pleasures." *Seattle Post-Intelligencer*, June 8.

1980 Lumbard, Paula. "News and Reviews." *Spinning Off*, March.

1980 Campbell, R.M. "An Air of Violence and Tension." *Seattle Post-Intelligencer*, February 29.

1979 Campbell, R.M. "A Lot of This and That." *Seattle Post-Intelligencer*, July 27.

1978 Tarzan, Deloris. "Fine Shows in 'Final Day'." *Seattle Times*, April 25.

1978 Campbell, R.M. "Jones' Work Not As It Seems." *Seattle Post-Intelligencer*, April 23.

1978 Winn, Steven. "Paintings by Fay Jones." *The Weekly* (Seattle, WA), April 19.

1978 Shere, Charles. "Gallery-Going in the Northwest." *Oakland Tribune*, January 29.

1977 "Warshal's Mural." Art in Seattle Public Places #2, *Seattle Arts*, May.

1976 Campbell, R.M. "A Trio of Solo Exhibitions." *Seattle Post-Intelligencer*, October 8.

1976 Tarzan, Deloris. "Figures Show Fantasy, Process at Seders, Manolides, Matheson." *Seattle Times*, October 5.

1975 Orlock, Carol. "Paintings, Drawings and Ceramics by Northwest Artists." *Artweek*, January 4.

1972 McG, Joy. "New Show at Art Gallery." *Ellensburg Daily Record*, May 8.

1970 Vorhees, John. "Acrylics, Sculpture Work Well at Seders." *Seattle Times*, November 10.

Boise Art Museum Board Of Trustees 1996-1997

Boise Art Museum Staff

Dennis O'Leary
Executive Director

Nancy McDaniel
Associate Director

Collections And Exhibitions

Sandy Harthorn
Curator of Exhibitions

Andrea Potochick
Curator of Education

Kathleen Bettis
Registrar

Cynthia Sewell
Curatorial Assistant

Ron Walker
Preparator

Administration

Laura Cobb
Development Assistant

Merita Nate
Receptionist

Liz Roberts
Special Events Coordinator

Lester Wyer
Accounting and Computer Systems Coordinator

The Museum Store

Sally Ferguson
Manager

Catherine Rakow
Senior Sales Associate

Frank Goitia
Sales Associate

Christine Harris
Sales Associate

Credits

Editors:
Kathleen Bettis
and Cynthia Sewell

Design:
Geoffrey Beard,
Graphic Resource, Inc.
Boise, Idaho

Printer:
Graphic Art Center
Portland, Oregon

Photographs:
David Anderson, p. 32
Eduardo Calderón, cover, pp. 6, 29, 33, 40, 44, 46, 47, 48, 49, 51, 52, 54, 55, 56
Chris Eden, pp. 22, 37, 43
Maja Kihlstedt, p. 10
Spike Mafford, pp. 41, 42, 45, 53,